PROTECTING CHILDREN, CREATING CITIZENS

Participatory Child Protection Practice in Norway and the United States

Katrin Križ

P

First published in Great Britain in 2022 by

Policy Press, an imprint of
Bristol University Press
University of Bristol
1-9 Old Park Hill
Bristol
BS2 8BB
UK
t: +44 (0)117 954 5940
e: bup-info@bristol.ac.uk

Details of international sales and distribution partners are available at
policy.bristoluniversitypress.co.uk

Cover design: Robin Hawes
Front cover image: istock/gavran333

This book is dedicated to all children

Contents

List of figures and tables

Figures

Tables

About the author

Katrin Križ is Professor of Sociology at Emmanuel College in Boston, US. She earned a PhD in sociology at Brandeis University and a master's degree in international development and social change at Clark University. Her research interests lie in the areas of child welfare, the education of the children of migrant farm workers, and poverty. She has published on child welfare systems from a comparative perspective and on education for the children of immigrant migrant farm workers in the US. She is currently working on several research projects: an interview-based study of how employed undergraduate students in the US balance work with full time studies with Dr Janese Free, Emmanuel College; an interview-based study of the educational experiences of migrant children in the US with Dr Free; an edited volume on children's participation from an international perspective with Dr Mimi Petersen, Copenhagen College, and a large-scale comparative project on professional discretion in decision-making in child protection with Dr Marit Skivenes and colleagues from several other countries at the Center for Research on Discretion and Paternalism at the University of Bergen, Norway.

Acknowledgements

I would like to thank the following individuals for their emotional, intellectual, and/or practical support during the years it took to bring this project to life:

Mark Ahern, Katrina Bergeon, Kathryn Edin, Janese Free, Rose De Luca, Emma Frushell, Jenna Gaudette, Susan Bahia Jensen, Christa Kelleher, Joyce De Leo, William Leonard, Hans Križ, Marianne Križ, Bettina Križ and Oliver Križ, Gunda Križ and Nikolaus Križ, Neeva Križ Manandhar, Kaitlyn Moore, Noor Mughrabi, Katherine Parisi, Tarja Pösö, Brendan Quinn, Murat Recevik, Dakota Roundtree-Swain, Elspeth Slayter, Marit Skivenes, Sr Mary Johnson, SND, Inku Subedi, Lisa Stepanski and the members of the Todd Pond Book Club.

I owe great thanks to the study participants in California and Norway. Without their generosity and willingness to share their experiences this book would not have come into being. Thank you!

I would like to thank the anonymous reviewers who reviewed the book proposal and final draft manuscript. I am deeply grateful for their thoughtful and constructive comments.

I am thankful to Emmanuel College for providing me with sabbatical and research funding. I would also like to thank the Norwegian Research Council for funding the project CHILDPRO, which allowed me to spend a considerable amount of time on this project. The Norwegian Research Council Leiv Eiriksson Mobility Fellowship made it possible to work with Dr Skivenes in Norway to work on an early data analysis for this project.

1

Introduction

A few years ago, I had the privilege of working on a research project with Dakota Roundtree-Swain, then an undergraduate student at the college where I work. We examined the recollections of young adults who had been in out-of-home care about their experiences with participating in decision-making while in care. The study participants talked about their removal from family, placement in care, and parental visitations (Križ and Roundtree-Swain, 2017). Joseph,[1] an African-American young man who was pursuing a college degree at the time of the interview, said that when he was 12, he had called the local public child protection agency and reported being abused by his mother. He was subsequently placed in a foster home. Joseph described several situations when his opinion had not been heard by his child protection caseworkers. For example, the child protection agency wanted to reunite Joseph with his mother when he was 14. Joseph did not want to live with his mother, though, and told his case workers so, but he was returned to her anyway. He felt that the workers did not take his wish seriously because of his age:

> I was younger, I was 14, so I think it was really hard for [the child protection agency] to accept and notice that someone as young as I was could be insightful enough to see what was happening and to realize that ... the kid wasn't just feeling hate or just complaining, and to realize that they were in a toxic situation and needed to get out of it. (Križ and Roundtree-Swain, 2017, pp 37–8)

Joseph thought that the caseworkers perceived him as a problem that needed fixing. He described the child protection system as a factory treating children in care as objects that are produced in an automated, identical fashion, as if on an assembly line. He explained: 'I've always looked at foster care as a factory: ... we are merchandise on this conveyor belt' (Križ and Roundtree-Swain, 2017, p 32).

Joseph's powerful words about his experiences in care were the motivation to write this book. Dakota's and my project showed that the study participants' experiences with participation in child protection-related processes varied widely. Joseph and the other young people

Dakota interviewed remembered few situations when they had choices and could participate in decisions and many when they could not. They believed that children should receive information from their case workers so they know what is going on and can develop an opinion about their situation. They thought that children's opinions should be heard and given weight in decision-making processes. (I use the term 'children' to describe all children under the age of 18, including adolescents and younger children. I sometimes specifically refer to children between the ages of 12 and 18 years as 'adolescents', 'youth' or 'young people'.)

Goal and argument

This book aims to show in what ways child protection caseworkers employed by public child protection agencies in Norway and the US (California[2]) can create citizens by promoting the participation of children and young people like Joseph in their everyday practice. There is ample evidence about how professionals working in child protection systems discourage children's and young people's participation, as I will show in Chapter 2. My goal in writing this book was to highlight the participatory work that child protection workers undertake to promote children's citizenship while protecting them from harm.

I wanted to study whether and how children's 'substantive citizenship' (Glenn, 2010), their full inclusion into their community through participation, is accomplished in the interactions with professionals in child protection settings. I took this micro sociological, symbolic and interactionist approach to the study of child protection systems not to deflect from the arguments about systemic racial, ethnic and class oppression of children, youth and families who come into contact with child protection systems (see, for example, Roberts, 2002; 2008; Roberts and Sangoi, 2018), but because I was curious about what happens *inside* the system from the viewpoint of child protection caseworkers. I leaned on the symbolic interactionist tradition in sociology (Goffman, 1959) and especially the work of West and Zimmerman (1987) to show in what ways child protection workers 'do participation', that is how they promote children's participation in interactions with them.

Following the symbolic interactionist paradigm, citizens are understood here as individuals who are recognized as active participants both by those they interact with and by wider society, for example through legislation and public policy. My understanding of children's and young people's citizenship was inspired by an article on citizenship by Sherry Arnstein. Arnstein (1969, p 216) defined citizenship as 'a categorical term for citizen power. It is the redistribution of power that enables the have-not citizens, presently excluded from the political and economic processes, to be deliberately included in the future.' By my definition, 'citizens' are individuals who have the opportunity to participate in decisions that affect their own lives and the lives of their families and communities. They may exercise their power as citizens through participation in elections, engaging in community activism or membership in associations. They may also exercise their power through participation in everyday decisions in the family, at school, at workplaces and in interaction with state bureaucracies, such as the public child protection system.

Public child protection agencies are only one part of the citizenship piece, but they are a salient one in the lives of children and young people who encounter them. Child protection caseworkers, the 'street-level bureaucrats' (Lipsky, 1980) working in public child protection agencies, make very important decisions about children and young people's lives and provide children, youth and families with pertinent services. Children and youth must be able to participate in administrative decisions, according to the international standards set by the 1989 United Nations Convention on the Rights of the Child (CRC). As Joseph's example shows, street-level bureaucrats like child protection caseworkers have the power to create the conditions for children's and young people's participation. They can thus shape children and young people's opportunities to act as citizens. The aim of this book was to examine whether and how child protection caseworkers in Norway and the US help promote children's and young people's status as citizens by fostering participation.

I focused on child protection caseworkers' views of and practice with children and the organizational context in which these practices occur. Previous research on children's involvement in child protection-related processes has shown that it is important to consider organizational factors, such as the procedures employed by a child protection agency, to understand the degree to which children's and young people's participation occurs in child protection (see, for example, Vis et al, 2012; Vis and Fossum, 2013, and Vis and Fossum, 2015). I argue that, despite organizational and policy differences, child protection caseworkers in Norway and the US practise a participatory approach that promotes children's and young people's status as citizens. I demonstrate in what ways children and young people like Joseph can be empowered in their interactions with child protection caseworkers in child protection investigations and during service provision after removal from home. I will show how child protection caseworkers inform children and young people and encourage them to develop and express their own opinions.

I show that even in the context of a system characterized by unequal power relations between children and adults, a participatory practice approach is apparent. It is impossible to say how prevalent this participatory approach is across Norway and the US because my argument rests on a very small sample of study participants. My findings therefore cannot be generalized to other parts of Norway and the US, let alone the countries overall. However, my research suggests that the everyday interactions of child protection workers can be at the forefront of emancipatory practices – practices that allow children to be citizens as a result of interactions with adults. This is perhaps not surprising given the existence of theory and practice models in social work that focus on empowering, collaborative and client-centred anti-racist social work practice (Dominelli, 2018; Granosik et al, 2019).

I primarily drew on in-depth interviews with 28 experienced frontline child protection workers[3] employed by public child protection agencies in Norway and 40 workers in the state of California in the US. (More details on my sample, methods of data collection and analysis, and study limitations can be found in Appendix 1.) As the street-level bureaucrats working on the front lines of child protection policy, child protection caseworkers are in a unique position to provide pertinent evidence on the topic of children's participation because they interact with children daily. Their reflections on their experiences with children's participation constitute the empirical heart of this book. I also relied on prior scholarship on children's participation, some of it my co-researchers' and my own. I shall present this scholarship in Chapter 2.

Significance

This book shows how child protection caseworkers promote participation in the context of the tension between paternalism (the focus on protection of children and young people who are vulnerable to maltreatment) and participation that is inherent in child protection practice. Child protection professionals, given the nature of their work, approach children from a protective (rather than a rights) standpoint (Shemmings, 2000). This stance is legitimized by workers' professional authority to make decisions in children's best interests and protect them from abuse and neglect. For example, Skivenes and Strandbu (2006) and Vis et al (2011) have shown that children's formal right to participation in Norway does not necessarily translate into participatory practice in child protection. This is how Vis et al (2011, p 326) have described the contradiction between children's participation and the ethos of child protection among social workers in Norway:

> Although most social workers in principle believed that participation is appropriate and beneficial, it was apparent that child participation in decision-making was less likely if the case manager thought participation was unnecessary or posed a risk for the child. It is here that the UNCRC principle of participation as a child's right appears to conflict with a child protection service that is grounded in a child welfare ethos. In many child protection proceedings, children's rights to participation are set aside in focusing on children's best interests. When children's health or welfare is at stake, participation tends to be viewed as not necessary in order to make the right decision. (Vis et al, 2011, p 326)

The tension between children's right to protection from harm and their right to participation was expressed by James et al (2008) in this way: 'the "cared-for" may often find themselves at the mercy of the "carers" who control them, a process often leading to the denial of citizenship rights through social exclusion' (p 85).[4] This is how Archard and Skivenes (2009a) described the contradiction between children's genuine participation and the paternalism underlying child protection systems:

> The problem arises because the two commitments seem to pull in different directions: promotion of a child's welfare is essentially paternalistic since it asks us to do what we, but not necessarily the child, think is best for the child; whereas listening to the child's own views asks us to consider doing what the child, but not necessarily we, thinks is best for the child. (Archard and Skivenes, 2009a, p 2)

The participation of children in child protection-related processes can positively impact them by improving their safety and well-being and resulting in lower levels of foster placements (Vis et al, 2011). Vis et al (2011) conducted a review of 21 studies from Europe, the UK and the US to assess the effects of children's participation on their physical, mental and social well-being. They found that participation has a therapeutic effect by strengthening children's relationships with social workers and other professionals. Participation may increase self-esteem and children's sense of mastery and control and reduce stress and anxiety. Participation is beneficial because it reinforces the effect of other interventions by tailoring them to children's expectations and wishes. By promoting children's interests in child protection, participation allows for the development and implementation of more realistic case plans for the family and greater permanency for children. It keeps children safe by helping social workers discover and substantiate child abuse and neglect in investigations (Vis et al, 2011).

Other research evidence, too, points to the positive aspects of children's participation in child protection. The research conducted by Weisz et al (2011) about the risks and benefits of children's participation in foster care-related dependency or family court hearings in the Midwestern US analyzed the reactions of 43 children (between eight and 18 years) who had participated in review hearings in dependency court to the reactions of 50 children who had not participated. (The children who attended the hearings were typically older than 12 years.) The researchers found that children's involvement in the hearings was not emotionally harmful to them. The children who had attended the hearings had a better understanding of the details of their case and case plan. They reported more positive feelings about the process, especially when they met with a judge who provided encouragement, asked questions about children's preferences and engaged them in conversation (Weisz et al, 2011). Judges' attitudes and behaviours towards children in court hearings about their case can play an important role in facilitating children's participation. However, recent survey-based research with court officials in England, Norway, Finland and the US (California) has shown that courts could be more responsive to children, especially in terms of child-friendly language and time frames that are sensitive to children (Berrick Duerr et al, 2018).[5]

It is important to show the ways in which child protection caseworkers promote children's participation because the barriers to children's participation in child protection are formidable. Prior research evidence, which I discuss in more detail in Chapter 2, has made this abundantly clear (see, for example, Schofield and Thoburn, 1996; Thomas and O'Kane, 1999a; 1999b; Leeson, 2007; and Križ and Skivenes, 2015). The lingering cultural position of children as objects in today's adult-centric societies is one of the many barriers to children's participation in child protection today. The distinct and strong formal rights that children enjoy in the United Nations CRC and in law stand in contrast to the way in which governments and professionals working with children perceive and treat them. On one hand, children's rising social position has been well-documented in the scholarly literature on children and childhood: in sociology, for example, the scholarship by Zelizer (1994) and James and Prout (1997) represents early examples of research on the social construction of childhood. On the other hand, despite children's rising social status, they are still considered 'becomings' rather than 'beings'. Adults view children as the individuals who they may become in the future rather than focus on who they are today (Qvortrup, 1990; 2009). Child protection laws and policies, too, construct children in terms of who they may become, especially when policies focus on helping children develop into productive citizens in the future, as Lister (2006) and Piper (2008) have shown in the context of child protection policies in the UK.

A great deal of this book is devoted to child protection workers, describing how they create barriers to participation by drawing symbolic boundaries around the inclusion of children in decision-making. Symbolic boundaries are defined by sociologists Michèle Lamont and Virág Molnar (2002) as 'the conceptual distinctions made by social actors to categorize objects, people, practices, and even time and space' (p 168). These classification systems, which are based on cultural attitudes, create hierarchies between people that confer on some the status to exercise power and exclude others (Lamont et al, 2015). The 'participation boundaries' drawn by the research participants in this study involved situations in which they felt they could not speak with children and young people, for example when the participants feared that their involvement in decision-making might distress or retraumatize children and young people. Study participants did not involve children and young people when they could not verbalize their feelings and opinions because they were incapacitated by a severe physical disability or mental illness. A child's age served as a prominent symbolic divide between children's inclusion as well: children 12 years and older were typically viewed as individuals who should participate, while younger children were more likely excluded from genuine participation. There were country differences. Several of the US study participants described teens as 'liars' and 'manipulators' of adults. The types of perceptions that workers had of the teens they worked with were important because the participants who perceived them in negative terms did not appear to seriously consider their opinions. The participants in Norway were more likely to regard teens as participants because they viewed them as reasonable agents and strong enough to resist the child protection agency's interventions. Many study participants in both countries reasoned that an intervention measure, such as, for example, counselling or a drug use disorder treatment, would be fruitless unless teens bought into it.

Questions and concepts

I examined the views and experiences of child protection workers in Norway and the US to illustrate how workers in countries with two different child protection systems promote children's participation in their interactions with them. This book answers questions along three thematic areas: first, the study participants' views about why children can, should or must not participate in decision-making, and workers' justifications for providing participatory opportunities for some while excluding other children; second, the study participants' ways of doing participation; and third, the impact of laws, policies and organizational procedures on workers' participatory practices. Table 1.1 illustrates these thematic areas and research questions.

The term 'doing participation' spans the entire spectrum from fostering minimal participation by listening to a child's opinions and reflections without taking them into consideration to promoting genuine participation in decision-making. The terms 'genuine participation' and 'providing children with genuine participatory opportunities' refer to child protection workers listening to children *and* considering their wishes in their deliberations when making decisions in a case. For my use of genuine participation, I employed the definition put forward by Archard and Skivenes (2009b). It contains two important elements: first, that children's authentic voice is heard, that is, children must have the opportunity to develop, reflect on and express their own opinions about what they think should happen; second, that children's

Table 1.1: Topics and research questions

Thematic area	Research question
Child protection workers' views about children's participation	When do child protection workers think that children can, should or must not participate? What are the beliefs that workers draw from to justify allowing some children to participate while excluding others?
Child protection workers' ways of doing participation	How do child protection workers do participation in Norway and the US?
Effects of legal, policy and organizational contexts	How do laws, policies and organizational procedures facilitate or impede children's genuine participation?

views are taken into consideration in the deliberations about what should happen. Their reflections and opinions carry some weight in a decision that child protection workers make, even if their wishes do not necessarily drive that decision.

Hart's (1992) and Shier's (2001) rankings of the different levels of children's involvement are valuable in capturing the fine-grained gradations of children's empowerment through participation. Both these indices of children's participation in decision-making highlight the difference between a child's full empowerment through genuine participation, and a child's exclusion from power through manipulation by adults or participation that is mere tokenism. Hart depicted different levels of children's participation using the image of a ladder, with the lowest rank delineating the manipulation of children by adults. The highest level represents decisions initiated by children that are made in collaboration with adults, with children on equal footing (Hart, 1992, p 8). Similarly, Shier distinguished between five levels of empowerment, including: listening to children; supporting children in expressing their opinions and wishes; taking children's opinions seriously; involving children in decisions; and sharing power and responsibility with children (Shier, 2001, p 110). When all the levels are woven together, this constitutes 'genuine participation'.

Thomas's (2002) metaphor of a climbing wall of participation is pertinent in conceptualizing participation because it incorporates different kinds of life circumstances into a theoretical model of children's empowerment. The six bricks in the climbing wall conceptualized by Thomas consist of: (1) children's level of autonomy to make decisions; (2) their choice over participating; (3) their control over the process of making decisions; (4) the information children possess about what is happening and what their rights are; (5) the support children experience in voicing their opinions and wishes; and (6) children's voice in the setting where deliberation and decision-making happens. Thomas's conceptualization of participation adds to the other theoretical frames by differentiating between various kinds of children and situations in terms of capacities and opportunities: for example, children who can advocate for themselves may need less support to voice their opinions than children who are less assertive (Thomas, 2002). The support of a child protection worker may make all the difference for children who are less vocal. Thomas (2007) emphasized that, 'different kinds of participatory activities and relationships are appropriate to different settings and circumstances' (p 205). This is important in child protection because children meet child protection workers in a variety of settings, and their relationships and participation in them may differ. A child protection investigation setting differs from a case review meeting or a court hearing about child removal or parental visitation. During an investigation, child protection workers focus on assessing the risk to a child, often under extreme time pressure if the child is in imminent danger. In this situation, workers need to take the necessary steps to remove the child from home to keep the child safe.

I shall demonstrate that child protection workers 'do participation' in their daily practice (promote children's participation in their interactions with them) in five ways: by actively engaging children and building a respectful rapport with them; by providing information about the case process and the rationale behind the child protection agency's decisions; by giving children time and space to develop and express their opinions; by including teenagers as consultants and collaborators in important decisions, thereby creating 'youth citizens'; and child protection workers divest power away from themselves and towards children through 'recognition work'. Through this type of presentation of self workers convey to children that they recognize their wishes and see them as valuable contributors to decision-making processes. These approaches, which are common to client engagement in social work,[6] represent the core of the participatory practice approach of the participants in my study.

Theoretical framework

This study was mainly informed by two theoretical concepts: 'substantive citizenship' and 'street-level bureaucracy'. Children can become empowered citizens by being granted full inclusion into their community through genuine participation in decision-making. This status of full-fledged citizenship is called 'substantive citizenship' (Glenn, 2010). Child protection caseworkers, as the 'street-level bureaucrats' (Lipsky, 1980) implementing child protection policy in their interactions with children and families, can create children's substantive citizenship status in their interactions with them. Citizenship, Glenn (2010) posited, is more than individuals' access to formal rights. It is a social status obtained through processes of inclusion or exclusion, 'constructed through face-to-face interactions and through place-specific practices that occur within larger structural contexts' (2010, p 2). While these interactions, and the social structures they are embedded in, shape children's citizenship, children themselves shape their citizenship through their agency, as Bacon and Frankel (2014) contend.

In child protection, children's substantive citizenship status is constructed in the face-to-face interactions between children, their caregivers and adults working in the child protection system, including child protection workers, judges, legal representatives and other adults. Children's full inclusion in their community, their status as fully-fledged citizens, requires their empowered participation in these interactions. This includes their ability to express their opinion *and* have it taken seriously in interactions with child protection workers and others who seek to safeguard their wellbeing. When child protection workers empower children by giving them the opportunity to genuinely participate in decisions, they help children obtain substantive citizenship.

I am a comparative sociologist and have lived half of my life in Europe and half of my life in the US. The question of how the construction of children's substantive citizenship in child protection differs across child protection systems intrigued me. I departed from the theoretical standpoint that three types of context can influence child protection workers' interactions with the children on their caseload, namely: formal rights related to children's participation, such as the CRC and child protection laws and policies at the country level; practices and procedures at the organizational level (the child protection agency); and cultural ideologies about children, childhood, and children's participation, especially of children from families in poverty and children of colour. A similar approach to citizenship has been employed by scholars in the field of gender studies (see, for example, Haney, 1996, 2002; Korteweg, 2006). Gender scholars have combined analyses of the legal, policy and interactional levels when studying citizenship. For example, Korteweg (2006) compared how citizenship is gendered in welfare-to-work workshops in the Netherlands and the US. Her findings 'show the usefulness of understanding citizenship as not solely the granting or withholding of social rights through formal social policy legislation. It becomes clear that citizenship, much like social policy, is partly constructed at the street level, where particular bureaucratic practices are conduits for the signs through which citizen-subjects are recruited' (Korteweg, 2006, p 335).

It is important to view children's citizenship in the context of historical and current racial/ethnic and class biases. Historically, citizens have been considered those individuals who are part of a community that grants them the right to make decisions about their lives. This right assumed that human beings can make reasonable choices. This development, which has been occurring for over 250 years, began in the mid-18th century and wrested autonomy and sovereignty away from the power of the monarchy and clergy towards individuals. In the US, social groups other than white, property-owning men managed to gain human rights gradually by fighting for their rights (Hunt, 2007). Historian Lynn Hunt's (2007) argument about the development of human rights supports the importance of larger cultural forces in the creation of citizenship. She argues that people's identification with and empathy for others in very different circumstances were instrumental in the creation of human rights. Opposed to the rise of human rights were doctrines of exclusion, such as racism, anti-Semitism and misogyny. These narratives and arguments about innate differences between individuals promoted the exclusion of certain social groups, who were not considered worthy of fully-fledged citizenship (Hunt, 2007).

The notion of children's fully-fledged citizenship is historically relatively new. It is underpinned by the idea, embodied by the 1989 United Nations CRC, that children are not citizens of tomorrow, but citizens of today who possess rights in their present lives (Doek, 2008). The CRC is commonly cited as the legal platform that cemented the ideal of children's participation internationally (Invernizzi and Williams, 2008). Article 12 of the CRC established children's participation in 'judicial and administrative proceedings' (such as the processes in child protection) as an important policy goal. It declares:

1. States Parties shall assure to the child who is capable of forming his or her own views the right to express those views freely in all matters affecting the child, the views of the child being given due weight in accordance with the age and maturity of the child.
2. For this purpose, the child shall in particular be provided the opportunity to be heard in any judicial and administrative proceedings affecting the child, either directly, or through a representative or an appropriate body, in a manner consistent with the procedural rules of national law. (United Nations, 2020, n.p.)

I relied on the concept of 'street-level bureaucracy' to examine child protection workers' practices with and views on empowering children. The insights into the workings of street-level bureaucracies (Lipsky, 1980; Brodkin, 2012) underscore how street-level bureaucrats may affect the construction of children's participation. Street-level bureaucrats engage in (often unauthorized) informal, yet systematic behaviours (Brodkin, 2012), which build on their own normative judgements and ultimately create the relationship between children and the state. In child protection, child protection workers can either deem children worthy or unworthy of participation. Workers' perceptions of and attitudes towards children may matter to the extent to which children get the opportunity to participate, how children view themselves, and how others in society see children. In this regard, I was influenced by the insights of Thomas (2007); building on Bourdieu's (1992) theories of society, he argued that a theory of children's participation 'will need to understand not only institutional and legal context and processes, but the cultures and dispositions that underpin them' (p 216). The dispositions underlying child protection workers' interactions with children are what I am trying to reveal in this book.

The study of modern bureaucratic organizations, such as public child protection agencies, has a longstanding legacy in the social sciences: Michael Lipsky (1980), who built on Max Weber's legacy (Weber, 1946), defined street-level bureaucrats as the frontline service workers in public agencies who create public policy in their interactions with clients. In the face of the dilemmas that they invariably encounter in their work – such as budget constraints, unclear or contradictory policy or agency goals, time and information limits, and high caseloads– street-level bureaucrats may 'distort' public policy by dealing with clients in ways that undermine the original intention of the policy. They can do so because they enjoy a certain level of professional discretion. The actions of street-level bureaucrats then become the de facto policy (Lipsky, 1980; Brodkin, 2012). Brodkin explained that 'discretion is of interest not when it is random, but when it is structured by factors that influence informal behaviors to develop in systematic ways. It is these systematic informal behaviors that impart specific practical meaning to policy as produced' (Brodkin, 2012, p 942). One of the main goals of this book is to examine child protection workers' systematic, informal practices to find out how they contribute to creating children's citizenship.

One of the ways in which street-level bureaucrats 'manage' clients is by creating psychological benefits and sanctions. The signals that street-level bureaucrats send to clients about their dignity or worthiness (to participate, for example) can then positively, or negatively, reinforce clients' self-image. The labels that bureaucrats bestow on clients may have implications beyond the bureaucracy if a person's family or community treats the person differently after being stigmatized by street-level bureaucracy. The labels depend on (structural) factors, such as the bureaucrat's training, the social context in which the labelling occurs, and the presence or absence of other client populations (Lipsky, 1980; Brodkin, 2012).

In child protection, the power of street-level bureaucrats was evidenced by a research study conducted by Smith and Donovan (2003), who examined how frontline child protection workers in Illinois (US) dealt with the organizational pressures and institutional limitations in their work when reuniting children with families they had been removed from. Almost all the street-level bureaucrats the authors interviewed and observed in court used several strategies to deal with institutional constraints: they focused their energy on the parents they considered most demanding, thus prioritizing and cherry picking one group of parents while ignoring others. They denied the possibility that they could change parental behaviour (and therefore did not attempt to do so), or they attributed the failure of family reunification to the behaviour of individual parents by labelling them as 'resistant' (Smith and Donovan, 2003). While these types of behaviours may be functional for the individual street-level bureaucrat and the organization, they create systematic consequences by shaping 'policy as produced' (Brodkin, 2012, p 942). This is policy that differs from the original intention of policy makers. Such consequences are problematic because their impact can undermine both the original intent of the policy (Lipsky, 1980) and the legitimacy of the state.

Child protection in Norway and the US

A sizeable number of children in Norway and the US encounter public child protection agencies when child protection workers investigate children's caregivers for child maltreatment, remove children from home or develop service plans to assist families. Their interventions may include parenting support in the family, daycare, individual or family therapy, drug use disorder treatment, financial and housing assistance, and (if children have been removed from their family) foster, kin and residential care and adoption. In both countries, when a referral about child abuse and neglect reaches the public child protection agency, child protection workers investigate to assess the risk to the child and determine whether the child can safely remain in their home. In the US, after child maltreatment has been reported to a child protection agency, the report is either assessed for a child's risk of harm or, in some states, leads to an alternative or differential response. A differential response focuses on fulfilling a family's service needs with the help of the family and community services in cases where risk to the child is considered low or moderate. This could involve services such as welfare assistance and access to counselling. This is the type of response system of many counties in California (Reed and Karpilow, 2002; Berrick Duerr, 2018), the US state where the interviews for this book were conducted. Child protection workers in both countries make recommendations to the court (California) or the county board (Norway) to initiate a care order. This is a court order to move a child to an out-of-home placement (Berrick Duerr, Peckover, Pösö & Skivenes, 2015). It must be emphasized that the issues that child protection caseworkers in Norway and the United States face are similar – in both countries, workers deal with child neglect and abuse, and aim to keep children and young people safe.[7]

In Norway, child protection investigations were started or under way for 46,903 children under the age of 18 years by the end of 2016 – 42.2 children out of 1,000 children in that age group.[8] Also by the end of 2016, 12,636 children under 18 (11.4 children out of 1,000 children of that age) were in out-of-home care (Statistics Norway, 2017a). In the US in 2016, 3.5 million children (or 46.7 children per 1,000 children under the age of 18 years) were estimated to have received a child protection investigation or an alternative response. The number of children under 18 who were victims of child abuse and neglect was estimated to amount to 671,622 children nationally, or 9.1 per 1,000 children (US Department of Health and Human Services, Administration for Children and Families, Administration on Children, Youth and Families, Children's Bureau, 2018a). In the US, 437,465 children between birth and 20 years were in foster care nationally by the end of September 2016 (US Department of Health and Human Services, Administration for Children and Families, Administration on Children, Youth and Families, 2017).[9] This means that five out of 1,000 children in this age group were in foster care in the US.

Table 1.2 illustrates the main differences between the welfare state and child protection systems of the two countries.

Norway and the US embrace different types of welfare state models (Esping-Andersen, 1990; Arts & Gelissen, 2002) and child welfare systems (Gilbert et al, 2011). In the US, a liberal or residual welfare regime, the state only provides residual services to the most destitute through means-tested social programmes. Norway is a social-democratic welfare state that provides universal public services to children and families (Esping-Andersen, 1990), such as subsidized daycare for children starting at the age of one year (Norwegian Directorate for Children, Youth and Family Affairs, 2017). The difference in the two countries' social safety nets (wider in Norway than the US) and the extent of their public welfare provisions (more generous in Norway than the US) has implications for the variation in poverty levels and affects how the two countries score on the children's well-being index for OECD (Organisation for Economic Co-operation and Development) countries (UNICEF, 2013). This

Table 1.2: Legal, policy and organizational frameworks

	Norway	California
Welfare state context	• Social democratic[1]	• Liberal/residual[1]
Child protection system orientation	• Family service-oriented and child-centric[2] • Low intervention threshold[4]	• Child protection-oriented[3] • High intervention threshold[4]
Legal or policy guidance about children's participation	• Yes: legislation[5] • Yes: practice guidance[7]	• Yes: caseworker practice guidance[5] • Yes: court hearings[6]
Child protection workers' professional discretion	• Wide[8]	• Narrow: investigations • Structured Decision-Making (SDM)[9] • Case reviews: Team-Decision-Making[10]

Sources:
[1] Esping-Andersen, 1990; Arts & Gelissen, 2002
[2] Berrick Duerr, 2011; Križ & Skivenes, 2014
[3] Skivenes, 2011; Križ & Skivenes, 2014
[4] Skivenes & Søvig, 2017
[5] Berrick Duerr, Dickens, Pösö & Skivenes, 2015
[6] Barnes et al, 2012; California Courts, 2019
[7] BLD, 2009, cited in Eidhammer, 2014
[8] Berrick Duerr, Dickens, Pösö & Skivenes, 2015; Križ & Skivenes, 2015
[9] Berrick Duerr, Peckover, Pösö & Skivenes, 2015; Berrick Duerr, 2018
[10] Berrick Duerr, Peckover, Pösö & Skivenes, 2015

index includes variables such as material well-being, health, safety and education (UNICF, 2013). The US is ranked comparatively low on this index, whereas Norway is ranked among the top five out of 29 countries. Norway is ranked number two in children's 'overall well-being' (UNICEF, 2013, p 2), behind the Netherlands and ahead of Iceland, Finland and Sweden. The US is ranked as number 26, followed by Lithuania, Latvia and Romania (UNICEF, 2013).

The orientations of the child protection systems of Norway and the US differ. The Norwegian child protection system is considered a 'family service' system, and the US system is 'protection-oriented' (Berrick Duerr, 2011; Gilbert et al, 2011; Skivenes, 2011).[10] The differences between the two systems lie in the values underpinning them, and the way in which they approach children at risk. The main approach of family service systems is a preventative one; the child protection system seeks to provide universal public services to prevent more serious harm and prevent children's out-of-home placements. The Norwegian Child Welfare Act (Articles 4–12) stipulates that services to families must be offered first, or there must be evidence that they will not be useful, before a child can be removed (Ministry of Children, Equality and Social Inclusion, 2017). Children tend to be older in Norway than in the US before they are removed, but the proportion of children living in care is higher in Norway than in the US (Skivenes, 2011; Gilbert et al, 2011).

The US child protection system is oriented towards intervention once there is serious risk of harm to a child. The underlying normative principles of the US child protection system are the child's safety, permanency (continuity of care and connectedness for the child), and child and family well-being (Goldman et al, 2003; Berrick Duerr, 2011). These normative legal foundations were mainly established by the Child Abuse Prevention and Treatment Act 1974 (CAPTA) (PL 93–247) and the Adoption and Safe Families Act 1997 (ASFA) (PL 105–89). Public child protection agencies in the US focus on investigating child abuse and neglect in a legalistic, adversarial and often standardized manner after the event, allowing for less professional discretion than in Norway (Berrick Duerr, 2011). Decisions are made expeditiously to protect a child from imminent risk of harm. Once child maltreatment is reported to the telephone hotline in California, for example, a child protection worker must assess the danger to the child speedily. If the child is in imminent danger, then a worker must investigate the case within two hours. If the situation is not an emergency, then the time frame for the investigation is up to 10 calendar days (Berrick Duerr, Peckover, Pösö & Skivenes, 2015). According to Berrick Duerr, Peckover, Pösö and Skivenes (2015, pp 371–2)

> [t]he investigation/assessment process can take up to 30 days. Once a decision is made to take temporary custody of a child, the child is removed by the child protection worker … followed by a presentation of evidence to court within 48 hours in order to sustain custody, and further evidence must be presented to court within 30 days to detain a child longer and/or to impose a care plan for services.

Child maltreatment is prevented in Norway by targeting families in need of assistance through public services (Skivenes, 2011). The threshold for intervention is low in Norway compared to the US (Skivenes and Stenberg, 2015; Skivenes and Søvig, 2017). The time frame to complete an investigation in Norway is three months (six months in special circumstances) (Berrick Duerr, Peckover, Pösö & Skivenes, 201).

Children's participation in law, policy and practice

In Norway, the participation of children is firmly anchored in national law. In the US, which has not ratified the United Nations CRC, it mainly rests on state law and professional social work guidelines and practices within a child protection agency. Children in Norway have had strong formal rights as participants enshrined in law since the country signed the CRC in 1989. Norway turned the CRC into national law in 1991, explicitly using it as a platform to draft legislation about child welfare in Norway (Vis et al, 2012; Bårdsen, 2015; Berrick Duerr, Peckover, Pösö & Skivenes, 2015). The views of children aged seven and older must be considered in child protection in Norway (Vis et al, 2012; Berrick Duerr, Peckover, Pösö & Skivenes, 2015; Skivenes and Søvig, 2017). This is how the Child Protection Act 1992 (*Lov om Barneverntjenster*) formulates children's participatory rights related to age in Section 6.3:

> A child who has reached the age of 7, and a younger child who is capable of forming his or her own opinions, shall receive information and be given an opportunity to state his or her opinion before a decision is made in a case affecting him or her. Importance shall be attached to the opinion of the child in accordance with his or her age and maturity. A child may appear as a party in a case and exercise his or her rights as a party if he or she has reached the age of 15 and understands the subject-matter of the case. The county social welfare board [the body that makes care order decisions] may grant a child under the age of 15 rights as a party in special cases. In a case concerning measures for children with behavioural problems or measures for children who may be at risk of human trafficking, the child shall always be regarded as a party.

Children who are 15 or older become parties in a case and may be appointed a lawyer (Berrick Duerr, Dickens, Pösö & Skivenes, 2015; Berrick Duerr, Peckover, Pösö & Skivenes, 2015). Children 12 years and older must be heard in decisions about guardianship when a caregiver who is responsible for a child loses guardianship (Ministry of Children and Equality, 2016, p 23). Children younger than 15 years are invited to plan their care. The definition of children's best interests in the Child Welfare Act 1992 (Section 4.1) was amended in 2013 to specifically include children's participation in child protection with the help of an adult the child trusts:

> When applying the provisions of this chapter, decisive importance shall be attached to finding measures which are in the child's best interests. This includes attaching importance to giving the child stable and good contact with adults and continuity in the care provided.
>
> The child shall be given the opportunity to participate and steps shall be taken to facilitate interviews with the child. Children who have been taken into care by the child welfare service may be given the opportunity to be accompanied by a person whom the child particularly trusts. The Ministry may make further regulations regarding participation and regarding the duties and function of persons of trust. (Ministry of Children, Equality and Social Inclusion, 2017, p 13)

Since 2003, when the Human Rights Act was passed, the CRC has had primacy over any other national legislation in Norway (Bårdsen, 2015). As part of the Constitutional reform process from 2013 to 2014, a new article, Article 104, was introduced. It enshrines children's participatory rights in the Constitution (Bårdsen, 2015). The article reflects several policy principles found in Norwegian child protection legislation: a child's participation (depending on age and maturity), a child's best interests, protection and safety, material well-being, and family preservation.

Children in the US do not enjoy similarly strong formal rights to participation (Skivenes, 2015). This begins with the Constitution of the US, which does not mention children or families (Woodhouse, 1992). At the federal level, the 2006 amendment of the Social Security Act (Social Security Act, 2006) requires that children 16 years and older be consulted about their permanency or transition plans in court or administrative hearings, but practices vary by state (Social Security Act, 2006; Weisz et al, 2011; Barnes et al, 2012). The state of California, where the interviews for this study were conducted, has introduced its own legislation regarding children's age and participation in court: if children ten years and older do not attend their court hearing in California, the judge will inquire whether the child had the chance to appear in court (Advokids, 2018). All children are assigned an attorney who represents them in court (Berrick Duerr et al, 2018).

Children who attend hearings in juvenile court may work with a Court Appointed Special Advocate (CASA). A CASA is a trained lay person who volunteers to assist the child to get their wishes heard in court (Berrick Duerr, Dickens, Pösö & Skivenes, 2015).

The US has a decentralized child protection system. Each state interprets and implements federal child protection laws and regulations differently. Child protection is administered at the county level in California (Berrick Duerr, 2011; Child Welfare Information Gateway, 2018). In Norway, the municipalities are responsible for undertaking child protection work. They are tasked with providing services in the home when a child requires assistance and applying for out-of-home services when in-home services do not work or are inappropriate. The 12 county social welfare boards in Norway decide about involuntary child welfare services, such as mandatory daycare, supervised visits, and out-of-home care. They typically consist of a lawyer (who chairs), an expert member (a professional with expertise in child protection), and a layperson (Skivenes and Søvig, 2017). In Norway, child protection workers enjoy a great deal of discretion. For example, it is up to the case manager to decide whether to let children participate in planning meetings (Vis et al, 2011).

Child protection workers who investigate abuse and neglect in public child protection agencies in California are more constricted when investigating child maltreatment because they utilize standard assessment tools during an investigation. Many of the Californian child protection agencies, including the ones in this study, employed an actuarial tool called a Structured Decision-Making Scheme (SDM) for their risk assessments (Berrick Duerr, Peckover, Pösö & Skivenes, 2015; Berrick Duerr, 2018). Actuarial tools such as SDM provide factors predictive of maltreatment which workers score to provide an overall risk score (Ryan et al, 2005; D'Andrade et al, 2008; Berrick Duerr, Peckover, Pösö & Skivenes, 2015). The higher the point tally, the higher the risk in the case (California Department of Social Services, 2012). The Norwegian risk assessment approach, which differs from that employed in California, rests solely on professional discretion and knowledge: the norm in Norwegian child protection practice is to rely on individual workers' professional assessment of the situation. However, there are indications of a turn towards more systematic guidelines in the Norwegian system, such as the so-called Kvello method (Kvello, 2010) that several municipalities are now using (Skivenes, 2011). Several Norwegian research participants in this study mentioned employing 'The River of Life' tool, which allowed them to gather information about children in a structured manner during a child protection investigation.

Californian child protection workers are expected to follow a practice model that includes expectations about how children should be treated in terms of participation (Berrick Duerr, Dickens, Pösö & Skivenes, 2015). Many counties in California, including the two counties in which my study participants worked, practised an approach to meetings called Team Decision-Making (TDM) meetings, also called family team meetings. These types of meetings provide children, family members and other parties who know the family with a structured opportunity to be heard in a child's case (Berrick Duerr et al, 2015). Berrick Duerr (2018, p 222) describes TDMs like this:

> A meeting that brings together a family and other interested parties such as friends, neighbors and community members, with staff from the child welfare agency and other helping agencies (e.g., mental health, schools, etc.). Working together, the members learn what that family hopes to accomplish, set realistic goals, identify the family's strengths and needs, and make a plan for who will do what to keep the children safe.

According to Reed and Karpilow (2002): 'California child welfare workers use family group decision-making approaches to engage parents, children, and extended family members in making critical decisions regarding the safety and possible placement of the children and identifying services the family needs to continue or resume safely caring for the children' (p 39). Since 2014, California has implemented Safety Organized Practice (SOP), a strengths-based collaborative practice approach that emphasizes teamwork between the child, family, caseworker and community (Casey Family Programs, 2019).

Burford and Gallagher's (2015) research showed the positive impact of family group decision-making on children's participation. The researchers interviewed 32 teens in the US state of Vermont, most of whom were living in out-of-home care, about their experiences with the child protection system. They found that interviewees were very satisfied with the family safety plan and family group conferences. These types of meetings are part of a practice model introduced by Vermont, following state legislation passed in 2007 that encouraged children's active participation in case planning. While these meetings have great democratic potential, only few families in Vermont get to access them, as it is up to the discretion of the public child protection agencies to offer them. These are the results of the researchers' survey data:

> We note that survey data gathered at the end of family safety plan meetings and family group conferences, which were both introduced as part of practice reforms, indicate high levels of teen satisfaction with these meetings. In particular, the family group conferences (N = 132) have received significantly higher ratings by teens on items such as 'other people at the meeting really listened to what I had to say'; 'I liked where the meeting was held'; and 'I think the right people helped make the plan.' These meetings almost always have a higher proportion of family members and people of the family's, including the teen's, choosing, and fewer professionals in attendance. (Burford and Gallagher, 2015, p 231)

Organization of the book

Legislation and policies may express goals and ambitions about children's rights to be heard, but the everyday reality of children's participation in child protection lies in the interactions between children and child protection workers. Child protection caseworkers may contribute to creating children's citizenship by establishing boundaries of children's inclusion and exclusion. They may, for example, exclude children from participation because they perceive some children, but not others, as deserving of participation. I examine in this book which factors child protection workers perceive as triggers of children's participation and non-participation. I analyze how child protection workers said they involved children, and in what ways they reported producing genuine opportunities of participation.

Chapter 2 discusses prior scholarship about children's experiences with participation and analyzes the barriers to children's genuine participation created by child protection professionals in Norway and the US. Chapters 3 to 6 offer the main empirical contributions of the book. In Chapter 3, I analyze 'non-participation triggers' – the factors in a child protection case that lead child protection workers to exclude children from participation. In Chapter 4, I take a 180-degree-turn and describe participation triggers. These are the situations in which child protection workers heavily weigh a child's reflection or opinions when making decisions. In Chapter 5, I examine how and at what stage child protection workers facilitate children's participation. In

Chapter 6, I investigate how workers involve teenagers compared to younger children. In Chapter 7, I weave together the findings from the empirical chapters and prior scholarship to present my central argument about the presence of a participatory practice approach. In Appendix 1, I describe the methods of data collection and analysis used for this study and the strengths and limitations of the data material. Appendix 2 offers questions for discussion.

2

Children's participation as contested practice

This chapter shows that children's participation in child protection remains a contested practice[1] – a practice not yet fully embraced by the public agencies charged with keeping children safe. The term 'contested practice' here refers to a set of social practices related to children's participation in decision-making occurring in child protection, including decisions about children's removal from home into foster or residential care, out-of-home placements, contact with parents and siblings while in care, and decisions related to family reunification. These decisions occur in interactions between children, their parents and/or other caregivers, child protection workers and other professionals (such as magistrates, judges and lawyers) in different settings. These settings include children's home or school, the child protection agency, court or court-like settings and other environments. Children's participation in these decisions may range from children being uninformed or not thoroughly consulted to, conversely, children's wishes and opinions being heard, respected and given weight in decisions.

This chapter starts by describing how children experience participation in different child protection systems in Norway, the US and other countries.[2] I shall then focus on the barriers to children's participation in child protection, especially the role that child protection workers play in creating participation barriers. I shall show that child protection workers' lack of availability, skills, training and a respectful rapport with children present participation barriers. Workers' protective attitudes and safety concerns in high-risk case contexts prevent children's participation too.

Children's experiences with participation

Children in contact with child protection agencies hold a variety of opinions about participation and experience a range of involvement in child protection-related processes. The spectrum ranges from exclusion to full participation (Thomas and O'Kane, 1999a and 1999b; Eidhammer, 2014; Paulsen, 2015 and 2016; Arbeiter and Toros, 2017;

Balsells et al, 2017; Križ and Roundtree-Swain, 2017). Children can experience participation in meetings and court hearings as comfortable and useful (Thomas and O'Kane, 1999a; Weisz et al, 2011; Križ and Roundtree-Swain, 2017), but participation can also feel tedious, oppressive, intrusive and frightening. Children may feel intimated by formal meeting areas and the formal language used in meetings (Thomas and O'Kane, 1999a; Pölkki et al, 2012; Cossar et al, 2014; Arbeiter and Toros, 2017).

The research evidence points to limitations in children's participation in child protection in Norway and the US, especially for younger children and children who are considered at serious or imminent risk of harm (Festinger, 1983; Oppedal, 1999; Skivenes and Strandbu, 2006; Willumsen and Skivenes, 2005; Vis and Thomas, 2009; Vis et al, 2011; Vis and Fossum, 2013). Children often do not have the information they need nor do they get the opportunity to develop an authentic opinion. They may not be able to voice their views because of a lack of procedures allowing them to do so (Festinger, 1983; Hochman et al, 2004; Moldestad al, 1998; Willumsen and Skivenes, 2005; Magnussen and Skivenes, 2015). When children's wishes and opinions are heard, they may not count, especially when they go against the preferences of the child protection agency (Vis and Thomas, 2009; Vis and Fossum, 2013; Križ and Roundtree-Swain, 2017).

Thomas and O'Kane's (1999a) study on children's participation in case review and planning meetings in England and Wales from 1996 to 1997 has shown that children generally valued participation in these meetings. They wanted to participate to voice their concerns, garner support and feel included, not necessarily to get what they wanted. Children embraced different attitudes towards participating: some felt that children should have a say or more of a say; others thought that they did not need much say, or that they were fine with adults making some of the decisions; and a small group of children sought to avoid participation because they found it extremely difficult (Thomas and O'Kane, 1999b). Children said they experienced enough support during meetings but wanted to have more information about the purpose, the participants, and the content of the meetings to feel better prepared. Children felt that adults listened to them, but this did not mean that their views influenced the decision (Thomas and O'Kane, 1999a).

Research on Norway and the US has shown that children wish to participate in child protection-related decisions (Burford and Gallagher, 2015; Križ and Roundtree-Swain, 2017) and that they are not harmed when participating in family court hearings (Weisz et al, 2011). At the same time, research on case review meetings and court hearings shows that children do not feel sufficiently informed (Križ and Roundtree-Swain, 2017). Research showed that their views are not represented in decision-making processes that concern them (Oppedal, 1999; Skivenes and Strandbu, 2006; Willumsen and Skivenes, 2005); and that the outcomes of child protection-related decisions do not, for the most part, reflect children's wishes (Vis and Thomas, 2009, for Norway). Studies by Pölkki et al (2012) and van Bijleveld et al (2014) on children's participation in child protection-related matters in Finland and the Netherlands evidence similar findings.

For the US, the 1983 landmark study by Festinger on the outcomes of young adults who had been in out-of-home care in the New York area between 1970 and 1975 first established the fact that children did not participate as much as they wished in important decisions related to their foster placements (Festinger, 1983). These decisions included visits with parents and siblings, where to move to, and which school to attend. The young adults who Festinger interviewed stated that they would have wanted more information about why they were placed in care and why they were moved from one foster home to another. They emphasized that the rapport between children and their social workers was pivotal in helping children understand their experiences while in care: workers who listened and were direct, informative, knowledgeable, mature and responsive were mentioned as most helpful in that respect (Festinger, 1983). Hochman et al (2004) also found that children who were placed in foster care did not feel sufficiently informed when they entered care. Children found the child protection jargon difficult to understand and needed more information on timetables and regulations of foster care. Children experienced 'few opportunities to ask questions, voice opinions or receive age appropriate guidance' (Hochman et al, 2004, p 9). Burford and Gallagher's (2015) study found that, '[y]oung people described those times when they didn't know what was happening and couldn't get workers or family to respond to them with information they thought was necessary as among their worst experiences' (p 246). The review of research on children's experiences in out-of-home care by Fox and Berrick Duerr (2006) concluded that many children are excluded from decisions in case planning. Children's age and unique history play a crucial role in the extent to and the ways in which they are involved. Block et al's (2010) study of the knowledge and attitudes of children who had participated in family court hearings in the US showed the limits of children's participation in court. The researchers found that over a third of children (37 per cent) felt unheard or not believed.

Over half of the children they surveyed (54 per cent) did not know what the outcome of their court hearing was.

In a 2017 study, Križ and Roundtree-Swain found that children in care were often not informed about child protection processes. The participants in the study recalled a range of experiences with participation: there were situations when they felt that they were informed, could voice their opinion and/or influence decision-making. All also recounted situations when they felt confused, scared and at a loss because they had not received information about what was happening. This was especially the case when they were first removed from home and entered care.[3] In situations when children wanted to remain with or visit their parents while their caseworker considered it unsafe, children felt unheard (Križ and Roundtree-Swain, 2017).

Norway and the US are not entirely different when it comes to children's participation in child protection-related processes (Berrick Duerr, Dickens, Pösö & Skivenes, 2015) despite differences in legislation about children's rights and the orientations of child protection systems (Gilbert et al, 2011; Križ and Skivenes, 2015), as shown in Chapter 1. Berrick Duerr, Dickens, Pösö & Skivenes (2015), who conducted a survey-based study on child protection workers' attitudes towards children's involvement in four countries, including Norway and California, concluded that, '[t]he role of children as active agents in child welfare processes is still evolving, albeit slowly, in California. Children are not necessarily seen as independent spokespersons, but as members of their wider family' (p 138). The researchers noted that the differences in child protection legislation, policies and practice guidelines did not yield significant differences in children's opportunities for participation. A Norwegian study by Oppedal (1999) found that, of the 297 children in out-of-home care whose cases they analyzed, only 21 per cent of the children aged seven to 11 years and 52 per cent of older children could represent their views in child protection-related meetings. Skivenes and Strandbu (2006) noted in their study about children's participation in the Norwegian child protection system: 'although Norway and other states give children strong participation rights, they have not made adequate arrangements for including children as actual participants' (p 15). Their research on children's participation in child protection meetings concluded that children were not given the opportunity to make their voice heard. Similarly, Vis et al (2011) stated that 'effective child participation in child protection proceedings has proved difficult in Norway' (p 325).

Willumsen and Skivenes (2005) studied the meetings of children, adults and child protection professionals and reviewed the cases of two young people residing in residential care. They found that children's views were excluded in these meetings. The researchers examined the degree to which children and adults were involved in the case review process and the interpersonal power dynamics between group members. They described the cases of 'Jane' and 'Tom' – two 14-year-old children who experienced neglect and abuse and suffered from psychosocial problems. This study revealed that both the children and their families received different amounts of representation. Not everyone who could participate did, especially Tom, who was not present in the meetings, nor was a spokesperson appointed to represent his views. The professionals did not establish any formal procedures for equalizing power imbalances between children and adults; however, they did make efforts to facilitate communication through active listening, follow-up questions, and they treated Jane and the parents respectfully. The authors concluded that the views of all parties should be sought in such meetings, the size of a group needs to be flexible depending on the meeting's purpose, and, most importantly, there must be formal procedures in place to ensure the inclusion of all parties (see also Holland and O'Neill, 2006).

Ulvik (2015), who analyzed 55 conversations between children and child protection workers in Norway, found that conversations did not always involve children's participation: for example, workers did not seek consent from children to start a conversation about a specific topic or occurrence. They communicated to children what their everyday life *should* be like, thereby conveying a message about normative expectations and not allowing for deviating ones – an obstacle to workers exploring children's viewpoints. Ulvik, similarly to Archard and Skivenes (2009b), found that the least common type of conversation was one where child protection workers explored the meaning of what children were saying.

Magnussen and Skivenes (2015) examined care order rulings by Norwegian county social welfare boards to analyze how children participated in decision-making. The study, which analyzed 53 written care order rulings on cases involving children between the ages of five and 11 between 2007 and 2013, found that in 70 per cent of the cases, the boards mentioned the children's opinion, with frequency of such disclosure increasing in 2012 to 2013. In only 15 per cent of these cases did the board elaborate on children's opinion. Further assessment of their opinion was found in 13 per cent of cases. When the board thoroughly considered children's view, they considered: the consistency of children's opinion, authenticity of statements, clarity of opinion, children's trustworthiness, and the relationship between children's opinion and level of risk. In total, 41 per cent of children were not heard. In 11 per cent of the cases, children's views were not mentioned in the board's arguments, and in 30 per cent the report did not mention children's opinion when reasoning the decision. This suggests that children's views of their situation did not figure strongly in the reasoning and argumentation process of the county boards.

Vis and Fossum (2013) found similarly low levels of the impact of children's wishes and opinions on child protection decision-making in Norway. The researchers assessed whether children got what they wanted in court by examining the outcome of court hearings and child welfare boards' decisions about custody and parental visitations in child protection cases. They analyzed 151 cases from 11 regional social welfare board archives in 2011 that included children between the ages of six and 14 years. In 39 per cent of the cases, court rulings coincided with children's wishes. They found that what children wanted and what they got depended on the extent to which their views coincided with those of the child protection agencies: children were most likely to get what they wanted if they lived in out-of-home care and did not want to move. The researchers found that children's views were effective in blocking decisions about visits but less effective when children asked for a specific change (Vis and Fossum, 2013).

Child protection workers' involvement of children

Comparative research on how child protection workers in Norway and the US view and approach children's participation in their work demonstrated a variety of attitudes and approaches (Križ and Skivenes, 2015). There is a group of workers in each country who embrace genuine participation of children, another group who fall in the middle and a small group of workers who exclude children from genuine participation (Archard and Skivenes, 2009b; Križ and Skivenes, 2015). These analyses evidence the existence of protective, paternalistic attitudes among some child protection workers and show the importance of age as a watershed to children's participation: in both countries, older children are more likely to be given the opportunity to participate than younger children (Archard and Skivenes, 2009b; Berrick Duerr et al, 2015; Križ and Skivenes, 2015; Skivenes, 2015).

Archard and Skivenes (2009b) drew on interview data with the same Norwegian sample of child protection workers as this book to analyze to what degree child protection workers give children the opportunity to participate in Norway and England. They found that workers embrace a range of views about how children can and should participate, including a protective attitude that precludes participation. They examined the reasons workers gave for children's participation and found that over half of the Norwegian workers and about a quarter of the English workers were likely to view hearing children as a fundamental right. (This may reflect Norway's adoption of the CRC into national legislation.) They found that workers showed sensitivity and skills in soliciting children's opinions and providing information. Some workers understood participation primarily as providing information to children about the process or an outcome of a decision that adults had already made. Others embraced an instrumentalist attitude by expressing that children's participation leads to better 'outcomes' (Archard and Skivenes, 2009b, p 396). Some workers only viewed children's participation as a tool to obtain children's compliance with a decision about services made by adults. One group of workers, consisting of the workers embracing a protective attitude, did not embrace children's participation because they thought that giving children a choice would place too much of a burden on them. None of the workers mentioned participation as an important vehicle towards allowing a child to develop an authentic opinion (Archard and Skivenes, 2009b).

Križ and Skivenes' (2015) comparative study analyzed the views of and experiences with children's participation of 91 child protection workers in England, Norway and the US (California). This study drew on interview data from the same sample of workers as quoted in this book but analyzed the responses to a different interview question (Križ and Skivenes, 2015). The study showed an evolving core understanding and practice of children's genuine participation across countries; however, the authors found variation in the degree to which workers conceptualized children's participation as empowerment: while none of the Norwegian workers understood participation as tokenism, manipulation or decoration (defined in that study as children being informed about the decision-making process but not playing a role in it), 35 per cent of workers in California did. In short, a larger group of workers in California than Norway conceptualized a type of participation that is a far cry from empowering children (Križ and Skivenes, 2015). The study detected protective or paternalistic views suggesting that children should be protected from participation because of its potentially harmful effects on them. The authors found that some of the workers in Norway and California understood participation as a necessary or important step in gathering information during an investigation into the level of risk to the child. This was a more prevalent theme in the Californian data, perhaps because of the specificity of the Californian sample. Many of the Californian study participants worked in emergency response units and were charged with investigating imminent risk of harm to a child. This finding suggests that the extent of workers' promotion of children's genuine participation is stage-dependent: at the front end of the case, where time is pressing – by law, workers in California have ten days to investigate and assess the level of risk to a child following a referral (and only two hours if children are in imminent danger) (Berrick Duerr et al, 2015b) – genuine participation is less important than gathering information from children to determine whether they must be removed from home. Because preparations for care order proceedings (court hearings to determine whether a child should be moved into out-of-home care) are more time-limited in California, 'information gathering is intense at this stage of the process' (p 634), according to Berrick Duerr et al (2017).

Berrick Duerr, Dickens, Pösö & Skivenes (2015) demonstrated that a system's orientation (protection-oriented in the US versus family support-oriented in Norway) affects child protection workers' approaches to promoting children's involvement. The existence of established participatory procedures, such as TDM in the US, and financial and time resources also matter (Berrick Duerr, Dickens, Pösö & Skivenes 2015). The researchers' four-country study on England, the US (California), Finland and Norway asked child protection workers to react to a case vignette in which the risk to the child, a five-year-old boy, was described as high, and the child protection agency had started preparations for care order proceedings (Berrick Duerr, Dickens, Pösö & Skivenes, 2015). The survey respondents were asked to state to what degree they would provide information to the child about the care order preparations, gather information from the child, and include the child in decision-making. They were asked how they would react if the boy were 11 years old (instead of five). The study showed the willingness of most workers in all the countries to involve children and the effect of age on participation: a large majority of workers in the four countries stated that they would involve both the five-year-old and the 11-year-old early in the process, but more so the 11-year-old. The Californian child protection workers answered similarly about talking with a child early in the process for the five- and 11-year-old (89 per cent and 91 per cent respectively). Norwegian workers were significantly less likely to be willing to involve the five-year-old (81 per cent versus 91 per cent for the 11-year-old). The Norwegian workers were more likely than their Californian counterparts to wish to discern the child's needs for help and support. Workers in California, more so than their Norwegian (and English and Finnish) counterparts, typically wanted to gather information from children but were less likely to provide information. The Californian respondents were more likely to ask children about their preferences about a future placement. The authors contributed the latter to the expansion of the participatory practices related to Family Group Decision-Making and TDM in California, which give all family members the opportunity to express their wishes about children's placement. The protective focus of the US child protection system (Berrick Duerr, 2011) and the time constraints of child protection workers in California during investigations, which may not allow them to focus on keeping the child fully informed, may account for Californian child protection workers' focus on gathering, rather than providing information (Berrick Duerr, Peckover, Pösö & Skivenes, 2015).

Another recent survey-based study that sought responses from child protection workers in England, Norway and California about a case vignette involving children of different age groups showed that a child's age mattered to Norwegian workers: the data evidenced a protective and paternalistic attitude towards the younger children, and an attitude focused on autonomy and self-determination towards the older children (15 years) (Skivenes, 2015).

Barriers to children's participation

Figure 2.1 summarizes the barriers to children's participation. I shall first discuss the barriers related to children, child protection workers and case contexts before describing organizational and systemic hurdles.

Children's age and lack of information

Age is an important factor that determines the extent of children's genuine participation (Vis and Thomas, 2009; Paulsen, 2015, 2016; Skivenes, 2015; see Shemmings, 2000 for the UK and Balsells et al, 2017 for Spain). Vis and Thomas (2009) studied 43 cases of 16 Norwegian case managers in which the caseworkers had spoken with children between the ages of seven and 12 years. The researchers analyzed information about the impact of case characteristics on participation and the factors that determined children's participation. They found that most children younger than ten experienced lower levels of participation in decision-making overall, whereas most older children experienced higher levels. The case managers said that children had a positive experience with the participation process in 65 per cent of the cases, a neutral one in 33 per cent, and a negative one in two per cent. Half (46.5 per cent) of all the cases manifested

Figure 2.1: Barriers to children's participation

Children:

- Age and maturity
- Intimidation
- Lack of information and understanding
- Lack of rapport with case worker
- Loyalty conflicts

Workers and case contexts:

- Lack of availability, confidence, rapport with child (respect and recognition), skills and training
- Negative labelling of the child
- Protective attitudes
- Safety concerns in high-risk context

Child protection organization and system:

- Case load
- Expert involvement
- Lack of formal criteria and procedures for involvement and meetings
- Organization of out-of-home care (Norway)
- Protection orientation
- Time pressure

higher levels of participation: a child had some understanding of what was happening, had expressed their opinions, and had had an impact on the decision. Case managers reported gaining increasing knowledge about children's wishes from all the cases they defined as 'participation' and most of those they defined as 'non-participation' (children were informed, understood what was going on and expressed their wishes but their opinion did not affect the decision); however, their knowledge of children's wishes did not translate into impact on the decision: 'consulting with children and ensuring their participation are not the same thing', Vis and Thomas (2009, p 163) concluded. Paulsen (2015; 2016), who interviewed 45 youths aged 16 to 26 years in Norway, also found that age played a role in children's participation: older children were more likely to be present in meetings and conversations. Paulsen noted that, even though the frequency of participation increased for her study participants the older they got, this did not necessarily mean they were able to participate in the meetings (Paulsen, 2015; 2016).

Magnussen and Skivenes's (2015) study demonstrated that age mattered when children were heard in care order decisions made by county boards in Norway: the opinions of children aged five and six years were more likely to be excluded. Children younger than seven years who can form their own opinions must be heard, according to Norwegian law. The researchers showed that decision-makers on county boards excluded some children without providing any justification. In 18 out of the 53 cases analyzed by the researchers, no spokesperson was appointed for the child. Most of these children without a voice were under eight years old. The authors found that, in most case descriptions, the children's perspective was represented by an adult, not by children themselves, a representation that effectively excluded children's voices (Magnussen and Skivenes, 2015).

Children's lack of access to information about child protection-related processes in general and their case in specific represents a significant barrier to participation (Thomas and O'Kane, 1999a; Pinkney, 2011; Pölkki et al, 2012; Eidhammer, 2014; van Bijleveld et al, 2014; Burford and Gallagher, 2015; Balsells et al, 2017; Križ and Roundtree-Swain, 2017; Mateos et al, 2017). Eidhammer (2014), who conducted one-on-one interviews and focus group discussions with youths in out-of-home care in Norway, showed that several of her study participants thought they were not informed about what was happening when they were removed from home, that the removal came as sudden and they did not understand what was going on. According to Eidhammer: 'What all these youth describe, is that things are 'suddenly' occurring and happening without them understanding the situation ... the Child Welfare Service decided things, and *then* informed them about what was happening' (p 55). The young adults in care in the north-eastern US whose experience Križ and Roundtree-Swain analyzed recalled the same experiences and feelings (Križ and Roundtree-Swain, 2017). Balsells et al (2017) studied the experiences with participation of children and adolescents in Spain. The researchers found that children's involvement during the assessment and removal processes in Spain, was limited, too: 'There are even occasions when they are not informed before the action [removal] is performed. As a result, children and adolescents may find themselves in a very abrupt situation without anyone informing them, and they may not be given the time or space to prepare themselves' (p 421). Children are not aware of why they are separated from their parents, especially during the risk assessment process; they do not find out what the separation from their family means, and do not know where and with whom they will live. They do not receive accurate information before reunification with their parents (Balsells et al, 2017).

Further, children do not necessarily articulate their wishes and effectively advocate for themselves – an ability that varies by age and cognitive and emotional development. They feel bored, frustrated or embarrassed or lack the confidence to express their opinions and wishes (Archard and Skivenes, 2009b). They may feel intimidated by their caseworkers. Arbeiter and Toros (2017) studied children's experiences with participation in South Estonia. The authors gave the example of a 12-year-old girl who felt fearful of a social worker who was escorted by police upon arrival at her house. When children do express opinions, they may say what they think others want to hear (Archard and Skivenes, 2009a), and they may try to avoid conflict with their parents (Vis, 2004). The research of Pölkki et al (2012) showed that children in foster care in Finland needed and wished for information about the reasons for their removal from home and for social workers' involvement in their life. They wanted to know when they could return home and what the plans for their future were. There were situations when the children did not want to be involved, for example in situations of loyalty conflict, when they feared that what they revealed to social workers might be harming their parents (Pölkki et al, 2012).

The experiences of the young adults Križ and Roundtree-Swain studied showed that a child's strong self-advocacy skills and clear, strong and persistent articulation of their opinion fostered their participation. Some children articulated their wishes and opinions verbally; others acted out to make their opinions count. Children felt that a history of compliance with the system and positive behaviour allowed them to make their voices heard (Križ and Roundtree-Swain, 2017). This finding parallels that of Burford and Gallagher: the teens interviewed in Vermont thought that if they were seen as cooperative and not defiant, they could expect more autonomy and freedom to make decisions (Burford and Gallagher, 2015).

Child protection caseworkers' attitudes and skills

Professionals working with children in the field of child protection do not always provide sufficient information to children, ask children for their opinions and wishes, allow children the time and space to develop their own opinions, and take these wishes seriously when making decisions (Skivenes and Strandbu, 2006; Archard and Skivenes, 2009b). Some professionals consider children too vulnerable to participate (Sanders and Mace, 2006; Vis et al, 2012) and perceive their participation as stressful or harmful to children (Vis, 2004; Skivenes and Strandbu, 2006; Vis et al, 2012; Berrick Duerr et al, 2015a; Križ and Skivenes, 2015). Child protection workers may view communication with children solely as a means to gather evidence in an investigation (Archard and Skivenes, 2009b; Križ and Skivenes, 2015; Berrick Duerr et al, 2015a; Wallace-Henry, 2015), or may not possess the confidence, knowledge and skills to proactively involve children (Vis, 2004; Alderson, 2008; Vis et al, 2012). Professionals who place negative labels on children may also undermine participation (Križ and Roundtree-Swain, 2017). Skill gaps related to a lack of training and supervision by organizations impede children's participation as well (Katz, 1997; Handley and Doyle, 2008; Križ and Roundtree-Swain, 2017). Eidhammer's (2014) and Paulsen's (2015; 2016) qualitative research with youths and young adults in Norway demonstrated that the quality of the relationship between children and their caseworker can make or break children's chances to participate. Eidhammer found that, when there was little contact between children and their caseworkers or when caseworkers were unavailable (because of sickness, vacation time, and so on) and changed frequently, children's participation in decisions was less likely. The latter is the case because a frequent change in caseworker precludes the formation of a stable and trusting relationship between children and caseworkers, as Paulsen (2015; 2016) has argued.

Research on children's participation in county social welfare board hearings in Norway showed that children's genuine participation is affected by decision-makers' views of children's authenticity, trustworthiness, consistency of opinion and risk to the child (Moldestad et al, 1998; Magnussen and Skivenes, 2015). The young adults in Križ and Roundtree-Swain's study said that their social workers' attitudes towards them affected the extent of their participation: the study participants felt that they were less likely to be heard if their social worker placed a negative label on them (Križ and Roundtree-Swain, 2017). Burford and Gallagher (2015) stated that:

> Importantly, many of the young people [in our study] had been diagnosed with single or more often multiple labels and many had long histories of taking behavioral medications. Their assessment of whether they could effectively stand up for themselves and voice their views was clearly related to these diagnoses and the extent to which they were viewed as competent by professionals. (Burford and Gallagher, 2015, p 248)

The young adults in Križ and Roundtree-Swain's (2017) study thought that social workers' knowledge and skills in communicating with children promoted participation. A respectful and trusting relationship between children and social workers was considered as a stepping stone towards participation. The latter finding corroborates earlier research by Bell (2002), Smith et al (2003), Healy and Darlington (2009); Vis et al (2012), Cossar et al (2014), and Burford and Gallagher (2015) about the saliency of a respectful and trusting child-professional rapport in encouraging participation. When Burford and Gallagher's (2015) study participants 'talked about "bad" social workers, the evidence cited was almost always about lack of competence, lack of responsive communication and contact, or arbitrary decisions' (p 242). The children interviewed by Arbeiter and Toros (2017) articulated that kind, helpful child protection workers who were motivational, frank and available were salient to participation. Children's interactions with those child welfare workers and other professionals who do not respect and listen to children (Thomas and O'Kane, 1999a; Pölkki et al, 2012; Cossar et al, 2014) and legal representatives who do not adequately represent children's wishes (Križ and Roundtree-Swain, 2017) deter children from participating. Eidhammer (2014) showed that adults in Norway (supervisors, professionals who evaluate a child's experience in foster care, the child protection agency, and foster carers) do not necessarily act on behalf of the child. This may be exacerbated if supervisors and foster carers have close personal ties with each other (Barnevernsproffene, 2011).

The principle of participation has been shown to give way to the principle of child safety in situations in which children are considered at imminent or high risk of harm. The (1998) study by Moldestad et al, which is based on interviews with seven judges in Norway, found that children's wishes were less likely to be heard in more serious cases of abuse and neglect, where child safety would take precedence (see also van Bijleveld et al, 2014). Moldestad et al (1998) found that the board gave children's views more weight when it had doubts about how to proceed. Vis and Fossum (2015) reviewed research on the relationship between organizational factors and participation and concluded that 'social workers' engagement, work climate, organizational barriers within services and social workers' priorities and attitudes towards children's participation' (p 279) are among the factors that affect children's participation.

A recent study on Norway by Vis et al (2012) identified child protection workers' attitudes as obstacles for children's participation. The researchers asked 53 case managers from 30 municipalities and 33 social work students in their last year in a bachelor's degree programme in child protection to complete a survey questionnaire that contained statements about children's participation. Their study showed that respondents considered a good rapport with children – one that resulted in workers knowing children well – an important vehicle towards communication with children and participation. Vis et al (2011) stressed that:

> although participation has the potential to promote children's health in several ways ... it does not automatically follow that participation always has a benefit for children. In particular, the relationship with the social worker and the way in which the participation process is tailored to accommodate children's expectations and abilities, seem to be of importance. (pp 332–3)

Vis et al (2012) discovered that the 'protectionism' factor represented the most important barrier to participation among the case managers they interviewed in Norway. This is how Vis et al (2012, p 19) defined the 'protectionism' factor: 'the action of restricting the information that children are given, the people they can meet with or the discussions they are allowed to participate in, with the intent to protect them from possible disturbing or upsetting experiences'. Vis's (2009) study of case managers' attitudes in Norway found that children were less likely to participate in decisions if the case managers thought it was not necessary or considered it a risk to the child. On the other hand, child protection workers' proactive attitude towards children's participation was found to be an important predictor of participation:

> the participation advocates are those who think that it is always in children's best interests that they get to give their opinions and that children should always be asked what they think before decisions are being made, because being part of a participation process is more important for children than being able to decide what the outcome should be. (Vis et al, 2012, p 17)

The social work students the authors studied were more likely to embrace this proactively participatory attitude than the (more experienced) case managers. Skivenes and Strandbu's (2006) research highlights professionals' protective attitudes and skillsets as hurdles to participation: the researchers cited language and communication barriers, the difficulties of conveying the real meaning of children's unique experiences, and adults' social roles as protectors and educators in interactions with children as significant obstacles to children's participation.

Organizational and systemic barriers

Barriers to participation at the organizational level include a lack of meetings in which children get to participate and meeting environments that make children feel disenfranchised and intimidated. Formal and rigid bureaucratic meeting procedures and other processes that do not allow professionals to build rapport and engage with children decrease participation (Thomas and O'Kane, 1999a; Willumsen and Skivenes, 2005; Vis et al, 2011; Vis and Fossum, 2015). Vis and Thomas (2009) analyzed which case-specific and process-specific factors affected participation in Norway. They found that the best predictors for children's participation are the number of meetings a child attended and the fact that a child is referred to the public child protection agency for reasons other than abuse and neglect. The researchers concluded: 'it is important for children to attend meetings in order to participate effectively. The odds of a child participating increased by more than three times if they attended a meeting, and by many more times if they attended two or three' (Vis and Thomas, 2009, p 164). Paulsen (2015, 2016) found that children's attendance at meetings does not necessarily mean that they will get the opportunity to participate; however, children's chances of participation increase when they attend several meetings. The study by Nord Sæbjørnsen and Willumsen (2017) showed that adolescents' participation in interprofessional teams may increase their participation, especially if the adolescents can form a trusting relationship with one of the professionals on the team. The teens studied by Burford and Gallagher (2015) in Vermont experienced family meetings as empowering: 'these teens experienced their family meetings as nonadversarial [sic]; even the two young people who said the meetings accomplished nothing ending up describing results that were perfectly in line with the stated purposes [of these meetings]: greater participation of young people and their families' (p 251).

Vis and Fossum (2015) assessed the impact of organizational factors on children's participation with the help of a comparative study of out-of-home care related services in Norway conducted in

2011. They compared the views of social workers employed in 11 residential care institutions who oversee transitional planning and delivery of services to the views of workers who investigate and plan foster care services at one municipal child and family services department. In total, they surveyed 87 social workers about their views on children's participation, service quality, collaboration between services and work engagement. They found that the social workers in the residential units found participation more difficult than foster care workers (even when the researchers controlled for workers' gender, age, and work experience). A possible reason for this is that children 'with severe behavioral and social problems are, in general, likely to be admitted to residential care rather than foster care. Establishing trust and building partnerships with children with severe social problems may indeed be more difficult' (Vis and Fossum, 2015, p 284). The fact that residential workers found promoting participation more difficult could result from the more rigid rules in institutional care (see Eidhammer's (2014) findings). Vis and Fossum's (2015) study supported the findings of research conducted by the Norwegian Directorate for Children, Youth and Family Affairs (2010), which showed higher participation in important decisions among children living in foster than residential care.[4]

Prior research suggests that expert involvement may reduce the likelihood that a child's wishes are heard in court hearings. Vis and Fossum (2013) found that 'when an expert assessment was commissioned, this reduced the probability that a ruling would be consistent with what the child wanted' (p 2106). (The authors conceded that this could have been because the cases in which experts assisted are more severe.) This finding corroborates a German study by Goldbeck et al (2007, cited in Vis and Fossum, 2013), which showed that, when experts were involved in case planning (as opposed to standard case planning without experts), children's involvement in planning interventions decreased.

A fundamental tension exists between the child protection system's principle to act in the child's best interest by keeping children safe and the principle of children's participation. Children's wish to be reunited with their parents may conflict with the agency's mandate to keep children safe by removing them to a foster or residential home. Research from Norway (Vis and Fossum, 2013) reveals that in these cases the principle of a child's safety is very likely to overrule the child's ability to see the child's wish happen (that is, to return home). The child protection system follows its ethos – to keep children safe and with their family (or reunify the family if the child has been removed). That said, children should, under favourable circumstances, still receive and provide information about their case and voice their wishes, even if the ultimate decision runs against these wishes, as Skivenes and Strandbu (2006) have suggested.

The principle of children's participation has also been shown to contradict the principles of protection and family preservation in the US. Joseph's situation, which was discussed in Chapter 1, illustrates that children's participation in child protection-related decisions may be contested because a child's wishes may conflict with the child protection agency's mandate to reunify the family. For instance, Joseph's wish to remain in out-of-home care was not heeded because the agency considered it in Joseph's best interest to be reunified with his mother. Children's views and wishes may conflict with the wishes of their parents and the system's principle that a child should live with extended family if they cannot live their parents, as Berrick Duerr (2018) has shown for California. In the case example provided in Berrick Duerr (2018), Alison, a teenager who was removed from home like Joseph, did not want to return to her parents, who wished to be reunited with her. In addition, the child protection agency, at least initially, did not try to find relatives who could care for Alison. In the end, Freny Dessai, the child protection worker who described Alison's case in the book, was able to place Alison with relatives, and Alison was subsequently able to rebuild her relationship with her mother (Berrick Duerr, 2018).

Conclusion

The scholarship on children's participation in child protection-related processes has demonstrated that children's participation is an evolving and contested practice. The contested and inconsistent nature of children's participation is a result of adult-centric biases in child protection systems. In both countries, child protection caseworkers view parents, not children, as their primary clients. However, rights-based, participatory and child-centric approaches are evident in both child protection systems as well. The paternalistic logic of public child protection systems plays a role: professionals working within child protection systems who are charged with the protection of children at risk of abuse and neglect, must, by law, act against children's wishes in safeguarding their best interests. This is the case, for example, when the public child protection agency decides to remove children from home to keep them safe, or to reunify children with their parents, against children's wishes. In these situations, children's wishes may not be given weight.

Children's participation as a principle has not been applied consistently across the board by the professionals charged with applying it (Thomas and Percy-Smith, 2012; Berrick Duerr et al, 2015a). Despite a legislative mandate and participatory practice approaches in Norway (Skivenes and Strandbu, 2006) and the US, the extent of professional discretion may allow child protection workers' biases about children's participation to override laws and practice guidelines encouraging participation, as research evidence has shown in the context of the child protection systems of Australia and Norway (Tregeagle and Mason, 2008; Berrick Duerr et al, 2015a; Križ and Skivenes, 2015; Skivenes, 2015). Child protection workers' biases may stem from a protective attitude that considers children as vulnerable and is based on the fear that participation may harm children (Archard and Skivenes, 2009b; Vis et al, 2012; van Bijleveld et al, 2014; Križ and Skivenes, 2015). According to Leeson (2007), 'adults who seek to protect children in care tend to see them as especially vulnerable. This can create a situation where their voice is not heard and possibly render them more vulnerable, as they are not represented' (p 274). Workers' biases may stem from their insecurity about how to implement participation. A lack of time, knowledge, and skills in creating participatory opportunities may also present obstacles to participation (Vis, 2004; Alderson, 2008; Pölkki et al, 2012; Vis et al, 2012). Children may find participation in decision-making difficult for various reasons and avoid engaging in opportunities to participate (Thomas and O'Kane, 1999b; Tregeagle and Mason, 2008; Cossar et al, 2014).

The research evidence on Norway and the US shows that a core understanding of children's genuine participation is present among child protection workers in both countries. These views exist alongside lingering paternalistic attitudes towards children that preclude their full participation. Cross-country research reveals that: a child's age is a factor that child protection workers in both countries consider when they involve children in decision-making; and that organizational characteristics, such as time pressures during investigations, can impede children's genuine participation.

3

Non-participation triggers

When do child protection workers think that children *can, should* or *must not* participate in a case? This is an important question given the prominent role that these professionals can play in fostering genuine participation for children by helping them develop and voice their own opinions and taking their views seriously. The aim of this chapter is to show child protection caseworkers' views of the factors that lead to children's non-participation. I analyzed the interview responses of 67 child protection caseworkers (28 workers in Norway, 'N', and 39 in California, 'C') who were asked whether they thought there were situations when it would not be appropriate to involve children in child protection-related processes. The study participants were prompted to provide concrete examples based on their practice. Their views and experiences and the examples of situations they described constitute the evidence for this chapter.

Workers in both countries perceived several reasons why children can or should not participate, as Figure 3.1 shows.

These reasons, which I call 'non-participation triggers', included: children's young age (the non-participant thresholds most frequently mentioned were infancy, three and four years); children's severe disability or mental illness, such as speech problems or a severe mental health issue that incapacitated children; and the possibility of negative emotional impact of the involvement on children. Study participants also mentioned the possibility of retraumatizing the child if they faced an abuser in a meeting and any imminent risk to children's safety. A few workers in both countries mentioned the occurrence of a crime as a non-involvement trigger, a case focus on providing parenting support services, or the child's wish not to be involved.

When child protection caseworkers in Norway and California were asked whether there were situations when they would not involve children, most of them were adamant in replying that children should always be involved; however, many of them then continued to qualify their statements by saying that there are instances when children can, should or must not be involved. Only a few workers simply said that children should always be involved, without qualifying their statement. For example, C26 replied: "This is child welfare, so I would think the majority of the time the child is the key factor. I can't think of one

Figure 3.1: Non-participation triggers

Young age:

- Children cannot process information and/or develop and articulate an opinion because of their young age.

Severe disability or mental illness:

- Children cannot process information and/or develop and articulate an opinion because of a physical disability or severe mental health problem.

Negative emotional impact of participation:

- Workers seek to avoid distressing or traumatizing children.

Imminent risk to the child:

- Children must be removed from their family without being heard because of imminent risk to their safety.

Table 3.1: Themes by frequency in total sample (n=67)

Themes	Norway 100% (n=28) % (n)	US (California) 100% (n=39) % (n)	Total 100% (n=67) % (n)
Young age	36% (10)	38% (15)	37% (25)
Severe disability or mental illness	11% (3)	28% (11)	36% (24)
Negative emotional effects of participation	11% (3)	36% (14)	25% (17)
Imminent risk	39% (11)	13% (5)	24% (16)

[situation] off-hand [when the child shouldn't be involved]". N22 said: "I think that the goal is that children should be involved, but it does not mean they should decide. I think they should always be given an opportunity to comment." Table 3.1 displays the themes that emerged from the data, ordered by the frequency in which they were mentioned in the total sample. (The table shows the themes that were mentioned by ten or more per cent of the participants.)

The same non-participation triggers were apparent in both the Norwegian and Californian samples. The frequency of the themes varied, except for age: study participants in Norway and California thought that children's young age was a reason not to involve them to a similar degree as older children. Californians were more likely to mention negative emotional consequences and physical and emotional disabilities. The Norwegian study participants were more likely to mention imminent risk to the child as a reason.

Young age

When workers in California and Norway mentioned age when they described situations in which they would not involve children, they discussed infancy and three and four years as the threshold ages for children's non-participation. Californian workers used two types of rationales to explain why children were too young to participate: first, many workers (n=10) explained that very young children (infants, toddlers, and children younger than four) were unable to 'understand'. Workers did not speak with very young children during an investigation. Most of the Californian participants who cited young age as a barrier to speaking with children were those who used examples of risk assessments during an investigation. Children's 'involvement' meant that they gathered information about young children from other sources. It is noteworthy that most of these investigators mentioned strategies they used to involve young children as well, mainly by assessing children's situation and determining their service needs in ways other than talking with them, especially by observing them as they interacted with their caregivers or siblings. A smaller group of Californian workers who mentioned age (n=5) thought that young children might be too young to be exposed to certain types of information (about sexual and physical abuse). If they knew this information, children would feel distressed or traumatized. A few participants in Norway expressed that they would not involve very young children because of their lack of understanding and ability to express themselves. In the following, I shall provide evidence for both types of the most frequent rationales related to age.

In California, several participants mentioned very young children's lack of understanding and their inability to develop and express an opinion as the reasons why they would not involve them. For example, C3 explained that, "if they're too young to understand or developmentally delayed and they can't understand, you obviously wouldn't involve them in a case". C2 put it briefly: "A lot ... depends on the age of the child because older kids can understand it a little bit better; the younger kids may not". A few participants in the Californian sample explained that they would not involve very young children because of their (age-related) vulnerability. They said they would withhold disturbing or traumatizing information from young children, or they would not allow them to participate in meetings for fear of further harm. For example, C19 thought that a child who is "too young, maybe four" should not be involved "if we're having a meeting about a mother's domestic violence situation incidence. Then the child shouldn't be there." C37 said that, "depending on the age of the child and the maturity level, there are some discussions or meetings where the child should not ... be present".

None of the Norwegian participants mentioned young children's vulnerability as a reason not to involve them. N6 thought that age would influence the degree to which a child is involved in decision-making. She elucidated: "If there's a three-year-old or a four-year-old, right, it's not that simple; then it is more about informing the child". N8 thought that "there is no point" in involving "the youngest [pre-verbal] children", but "as soon as they have language, I need to tell them what will happen in one way or the other because the kids realize that they will be moved somewhere". A little later in the interview, N8 mentioned that "the older they are, the more they understand. I think it's a little hard to tell where to draw the line."

Severe disability or mental illness

Three workers in the Norwegian sample (11 per cent) mentioned children with a disability (discussing developmental delays) and severe mental illness as cases when they would not involve children. N23 stated that: "I also think that adolescents, especially those who have developed drug problems or who have serious psychological problems, clearly, then adults must intervene and maybe do what they have to do regardless of what the young person believes there and then". Eleven workers in the Californian sample (28 per cent) considered severe impairment of a child or young person's capacity to understand and articulate (because of physical or mental health issues) as a reason not to involve them. C30 mentioned "a child who has mental health issues, who may be developmentally delayed" as a situation when a child should not be involved. She then elaborated: "I would do the best I could in interviewing them, but it would be more difficult as they're not able to speak as much". C38 replied like this:

> 'I think that if somebody had really, really significant mental health issues and they were going to be hospitalized and punching holes in the walls and were very violent and aggressive; maybe for that moment, until they got stabilized, maybe you wouldn't take their opinion into consideration at that time. But I think if that child became stabilized, then I think that would be a different story. So, it would be a very rare instance, but in an instance if they were a danger

to themselves or to somebody else, then maybe you'd want to lay off for a little bit.'

The next quotes indicate that workers might try to involve children with a mental illness but would not heed their opinion. This is how C21 responded to the question whether there were situations in which it would not be appropriate to involve children: "Yes, I think so. If a child is too young. If a child has mental health problems – I mean assessed by a mental health professional not my opinion, but someone said to me, he's schizophrenic or something like that. If a child has speech problems or is developmentally delayed." Then she qualified her statement, "I don't know if there's any time that you shouldn't ask them; I just don't know if you … should take [their opinions] into consideration. That's a tough one." C1 stated: "If a child is very emotionally disturbed or disabled in some way, it probably wouldn't be a good idea to involve the child because the child was severely traumatized or medically impaired somehow. All those … would be reasons not to weigh their opinion in decision-making." The responses of C21 and C30 indicate that workers may find it difficult to decide whether to heed the opinions of a child with physical impairments that affected the child's ability to speak.

Negative emotional effects of participation

Thirty-six per cent of the Californian participants and 11 per cent of the Norwegian participants cited adverse emotional effects of participation on the child, including fear, distress and trauma, as the reasons why they would not involve a child. Workers thought that children might be retraumatized or feel intimidated by the interaction with the child protection system and feel distressed or burdened by being placed in the middle of parental conflict, especially when there are custody battles. I shall discuss workers' rationales and their reactions to these two non-participation triggers in turn later in this chapter.

This is how C40 explained why she would not involve children:

'I have TDMs where, depending on what the parents are going to be discussing, it's not appropriate: it will retraumatize the child, especially like, for example, sex abuse cases. I have a protocol which I think is good, I only have to have the child say something happened in a sexual way, but I don't interview them about this so that they don't keep having to be retraumatized by telling that story to ten different people. Yes, absolutely, there's some cases where you have to protect the child, so they should not be participating in certain aspects of the case.'

C18, an emergency response worker, thought that, especially with sexual abuse cases, "you want to limit how many times the child has to report this". C18 said this when asked whether there were situations when it would not be good to talk to a child

'Very rarely. Sometimes it's obviously traumatic having to talk to me. But I did have a situation last week on a sex abuse referral, where it was alleged that this four-year-old girl was being sexually abused; and instead of my interviewing her and then having her be interviewed again, I sent her directly to the main hospital, where they have these forensic nurses that do these more comprehensive interviews and where they're better trained on sex abuse than I am.'

C37 listed several instances when children should not be included in TDMs because of the adverse emotional impact of their involvement:

'I think some substance abuse situations, if a child has not seen or experienced this, it's not a good idea to involve them in it if possible. Domestic violence very, very negatively impacts children. I mean children who witness domestic violence are sometimes more damaged than if they're physically abused themselves or emotionally abused themselves. It's a terror that may never leave them ... and it affects their behaviour as adults as well. It can. There are some decisions about where a child's going to live. I mean, if you have a whole family around with extended family members and you're discussing where a child's going to live, it may not be appropriate to have the child present for that discussion because there may be some family members who, although they may love the child, can't take the child for whatever reason, and it would be hurtful for the child. Maybe that's where the child really would like to go and it would be hurtful for the child. You don't want to damage the child any further.'

Workers stated that they would avoid children facing their abusers in meetings to protect them from distressing or retraumatizing them: C20 specified that: "The general rule is, if it's physical abuse, I do not have the child be present because I don't want the child to feel intimidated. So I think in that sense it's, again, it's for their safety; it's for their protection, and I don't want to retraumatize the child." C34 explained that: "If it was severe abuse, whether it's sex abuse or severe physical abuse, I would not have the perpetrator come to the meeting where the child would come. That would be too emotionally stressful for the child." C35 mentioned that, in TDMs, you would not want to expose a child to parents who are "emotionally unstable or irrational or psychotic or anything like that".

N4 thought that children's fear of the child protection agency might turn the interactions with the agency into an emotional burden. N4 provided recommendations for including children in her work by seeking their opinions through an intermediary whom children trust:

> 'We have some kids who are completely terrified ... [I] had a case a while ago, and the mum said that [her son] gets afraid when he sees the municipal logo in the mailbox. And there was one child, a child with a diagnosis ... in that case there was no point in talking with him. It was better if someone who was closer to him did it. And in a way the parents had asked for this kind of help for him ... we were to channel the assistance a little further and provide assistance, to consider it. It was not necessary for us to have direct contact with him. So it might just be a few such cases, where you see that they absolutely refuse, yeah right, that it is a burden for them. We are supposed to have a meaning and purpose in these talks, and not just to ... yes. So if, and if it is possible to handle it differently, that they can bring out what they think and feel, we are open to it. And some bring a teacher, or a support person, a friend or whoever it is.'

Workers in both countries sought to avoid creating loyalty conflicts for children by involving them because of the potential negative impact of conflict on the child. The quotes by Norwegian workers N18 and N17 show that workers seek to avoid distressing or burdening children by placing them in the middle of parental conflict in a custody battle. N18 said, "I think that I should involve or talk with the child in any case, no matter what; so I cannot think of any time I would not do that, but I think in cases of conflict between the parents, then I think that children should not get a say in what they want. It becomes too difficult for them." N17 told us that when children are removed from home, it is necessary to emphasize to the child that it is the county board, not the child, that has made the decision, "so that the child did not make the decision or that there's something about the child's statements that led to the removal – that is important to emphasize; and the child is not supposed to be used as an informant. This is about guilt and loyalty conflicts for the child." The following quotes by Californian study participants echoed these sentiments. C14 said that children should not be involved in decision-making "when you have parents fighting and competing with each other". She continued by saying:

> 'Parents are marginal, all things being equal, [and] I think it's wrong to put the child in the middle. And the younger the child, the less you should put them in the middle. Kids come into court and say, or come to you and say, "My friends told me that when I was 12, I could decide who I wanted to live with". And you might listen to them, and you might ask them, "Do you want to participate in making this decision of who you're going to live with or not? And either way is OK." So, if a kid says, and I've had kids say to me, "I don't really want to make that choice. I love both my parents", then I think you leave them out of it. You say to the parents, this is ... because one of the things that's usually happened in that situation is one or both of the parents are putting the kid in the middle and using the kid as a pawn, so I think you have to say, "I'm here for you, but you don't have to [decide] – the grown-ups can decide this".'

C39 explained how she worked with children in custody battles by deflecting the conflict away from children and back onto parents:

> 'We get all the shitload of calls [on the hotline of the child protection agency] about [instances] ... that happen to be custody cases, and where parents put the kids in the middle of it. So, you know, we're required to interview kids, which I do, and we'll talk to kids about certain things. But only ... to ... just ask them, "What happens with mum? What happens with dad?" to see if there's any abuse going on. But then not to keep bothering the kids or asking, "Well, who

do you want to go with?", because I do get a lot of custody cases where parents try to use us to get back at their other parents. Yeah, and they bring their kids into it, and I try to put it back on the parents and put it back in family court.'

Imminent risk

Almost half (40 per cent) of the Norwegian and 13 per cent of the Californian participants thought that imminent or acute risk to the safety of the child because of physical or sexual abuse was a reason not to heed the opinion of the child. N24 responded in the affirmative when asked whether there were situations when children should not be involved: "Yes, I think in sexual assault cases and in serious violence cases; in those two". N25 responded:

'Yes, for example in violence cases. In those cases, I've learned a lot the last time, with the risk and safety and everything. I cannot ask the child there, "Do you want to stay with dad even though he beats you when he's drunk?". A child should not stay with violent parents. It's clear that in those cases, or if they've been sexually abused or if there was any abuse at all, one should rather take a decision without involving the child.'

N28 replied in a similar manner: "Yes, I think in cases of abuse, for example, then I decide. There, I do not ask a child about what they want, or I could ask what they would want to happen, but it's only I who would have decided. Then I'm really protective." C6 voiced a comparable focus on safety first when she said that, "because there's a police action going on, so we're not going to involve them at that point. We're just going to get them to safety; but at some point, I would involve them." N23 embraced a similarly protective stance with a focus on the child's safety:

'These violence and abuse cases are the kind of cases where one should at least know what one does and must take some precautions. And especially when we are talking about sexual abuse or assault ... then I think that children do not have the precondition [awareness] often to maybe understand what is best for them. And ... the adults must make a decision regardless of whether ... the child wants it or not. For I've experienced that ... a child expresses, at least initially, strong reluctance to be moved out of the home, but was exposed to serious assault in the home ... But to ... shield the child from abuse [means] the child cannot always be heard.'

N19 mentioned "cases where you come into the family and let's say [children] don't have it so good here; mum and dad are completely unconscious and take drugs and beat [them]. I think security for the kids, safety for them, that is crucial. And then I do not ask." C23 recalled when she did not listen to a child's wishes in a case of sexual abuse:

'I have one case where the kid was raped repeatedly by a stepbrother and mum believed the stepbrother, and the kid wanted to go home. [The girl] was furious, and I talked to her and I told her what my concerns were, and that I didn't think mum would protect her, even though she'd tried to let mum know, and that I couldn't support it [the girl returning home]. She fired her attorney and she tried to get rid of me, so I just said, "no, I'm not going to do it".'

When describing these situations, the participants conceptualized 'involvement' as genuine participation in decision-making, not merely listening to children.

Several Norwegian workers used the adjective "acute (emergency) reports" or "acute (emergency) placements" (with the adjective "*akut*" in Norwegian) when discussing situations when they would not involve children. Workers expressed a sense of urgency and time pressure when making decisions in these situations. N13 responded by telling us about "certain types of cases associated with serious abuse and such issues, so it [the intervention of the child protection agency] happens ... quickly". N15 used the word "quickly" in her response: "We've got some clear-cut abuse cases where things happen a little quickly, for example, or I have to take protection into account, and the talking happens maybe more afterwards. It can happen that in those situations I have no opportunity [to talk with the child]." C5 clarified, "if it is sexual abuse, then I don't want children around the abuser, so you remove the child as quickly as possible if you determine that that's really what it is". N7 mentioned that while she would not involve the child before the removal, she would explain the reasons for the removal to the child afterwards:

'There are some [cases] where I would not meet the child before decisions are made. And it can be the kind of acute reports that are considered so serious that it is … Let me give you an example: I received a message from the emergency room that a child was at the emergency room with their parents with unexplainable injuries or bruises repeatedly and over a short period of time. Some injuries were so serious that the doctor thought that the child was being mistreated … When I think that this is so serious that the child should be removed, then I would not talk to the child about it beforehand. I would have spoken with the child afterwards and explained why I did what I did.'

This is how N2 described emergency placements:

'When there is an acute placement for example, then it is very acute; then we are not allowed talk to the children in advance … but I always talk with the emergency homes; they are supposed to be handling children in crisis, for example. Because it is often a crisis. So then there is just stuff that happens very acutely, so one tries to deal with the kids right in the situation. And I talk to them, but it is a bit like, I get them here and I talk a bit with them, but there's no point for them to be here so long. They should first get into a family, because that's what I want – that they [don't] stay here over time. So I want to get them into a family as quickly as possible.'

These quotes indicate that the ways in which workers involve a child in a case depend on the urgency perceived by workers about moving the child out of their home. In situations in which a child is at imminent risk of harm from physical or sexual abuse, workers prioritized protection over children's participation in decision-making. In these time-sensitive, acute, situations, the principle of child protection trumped the principle of children's participation.

Other non-participation triggers

Only a few workers in both countries mentioned the occurrence of a crime (9 per cent of all participants) or a case perceived as less low risk (7 per cent of all participants) as situations when they would not involve children. Ten per cent (n=4) of participants in California and 7 per cent (n=2) of participants in Norway mentioned a crime or police involvement as reasons not to involve a child. C10 told us that she would not involve a child involved in a criminal investigation: "For lots of the sexual abuse cases, especially for younger children, if there's a criminal case going on, I don't ask that because I don't want to jeopardize the criminal investigation". C5 provided a different reason as to why children should not be involved, which was related to children's vulnerability: "Certain criminal things where the parents are guilty of crimes, where the police are involved, you don't necessarily want the children to know too much about the negative part, [the parents'] involvement, so I don't think they need to know the whole truth when it doesn't involve them". Three Norwegian and two Californian participants mentioned cases with a sole focus on parenting support services as situations when they would not involve children. For example, when asked what determined the degree to which she thought that children should be involved, N15 replied:

> 'First severity [of a case]. So, let's say that here I have a little more like a lightweight case. It's a family that has gotten stuck in a little bad parenting pattern, but it's nothing serious, no serious concern for the child. But the parents could use some advice and tips on, okay, how can I get along again, for example, and such things. And [if] it's just about two parents coming here and getting some guidance hours for example, then it is rare [that we'd involve the kids].'

N7 answered that it was not important to meet with the child when PMTO (parenting support) was decided on as a measure for the family:

> 'In these situations, I will probably not talk with the child at all. It's not important for us to meet them. I have other professional agencies that give us a well-reasoned approach to why PMTO can be the appropriate measure. I meet the parents and apply for PMTO without talking with the child, but then I have others' assessments of the child's needs.'

Two Norwegian workers mentioned that the principle of minimal intervention in family life was the reason why they did not involve children. N10 stated that, "there are limits to what children should be involved in, and I also think minimal intervention in relation to them".

One Norwegian worker (N16) stated that children did not need to be involved in interagency meetings about logistical matters such as "staffing, routines, continuity, guidance". C4 reported that she would not involve a child in an investigation if the child was not present when the maltreatment of the child on her caseload occurred: "There are some situations when they're not in the home, like they don't reside in the home, or, depending on if it was one-time occurrence, they weren't present for that situation, but that's usually less likely the case". One worker in California said that she would not involve a child "if the child does not want to be involved" (C31). Similarly, a Norwegian worker (N4) thought she would not involve children "if you see that they absolutely refuse".

In addition to these non-participation triggers, the analysis of the question about situations when study participants would not involve children, revealed three types of approaches to how child protection workers handle information when interacting with children: first, an instrumentalist approach – *gathering information* from children, seen more in the Californian than the Norwegian sample (see also Archard and Skivenes, 2009b, and Križ and Skivenes, 2015); second, a paternalistic approach – *withholding information* from children, in situations where workers considered children too vulnerable to hear information about their case; and third, an empowering approach – *providing information* to children. Workers who used the latter approach often 'translated' information in a way that they thought children could understand. Prior research on children's participation has shown that children's access to information is salient to promoting their genuine participation because it allows them to develop their own opinion (Thomas and O'Kane, 1999a; Pölkki et al, 2012; van Bijleveld et al, 2014; Križ and Roundtree-Swain, 2017). In their study of youth's experiences with participation in the Vermont child protection system, Burford and Gallagher (2015) found that young people felt included when they knew about the next steps in a case and felt that they had control.

The Californian study participants' focus on gathering information from children could reflect the protective orientation of the American child protection system (Berrick Duerr, Dickens, Pösö & Skivenes, 2015). It may be because many of the study participants in the California sample were working in emergency response units and thus focused on assessing risk in a short time frame. Emergency response workers respond to referrals that reach the agency through a telephone hotline by investigating the risk to the child who was the subject of the referral. If the worker finds that the child will not be safe staying in their home, the agency removes the child from their primary caregivers and takes the child to an emergency foster home (Berrick Duerr, 2018).

A few of the Norwegian workers expressed the view that young children are important bearers of knowledge about their family; however, the focus of workers' responses was not on using this knowledge as a source of information in an investigation, but to provide information *to* children so they knew what was happening. In these workers' minds, young children appeared to be knowledge bearers who can process information even though they are young. This difference suggests that the cultural values about young children's knowledge and abilities may differ across the two countries. The Norwegian workers who described young children as knowledgeable and resilient echoed an article by US journalist and author Ann Jones (2016), who spent four years living in Norway. In an article in *The Nation*, Jones wrote that the US felt "backward" to her after living in Norway. One of the differences between Norway and the US that Jones described in her article was the way in which Norwegians raise children:

> [In Norway] at age 1, children ... start attending a neighborhood *barnehage* (kindergarten) for schooling spent largely outdoors. By the time kids enter free primary school at age 6, they are remarkably self-sufficient, confident, and good-natured. They know their way around town, and if caught in a snowstorm in the forest, how to build a fire and find the makings of a meal. (One kindergarten teacher explained, 'We teach them early to use an ax, so they understand it's a tool, not a weapon.').

Conclusion

This chapter has discussed what child protection caseworkers in Norway and the US considered reasons not to involve children. About the same proportion of study participants in the Norwegian and Californian samples mentioned a child's young age (the specific ages mentioned were infancy, one year and three and four years) as a reason why they did not involve children. However, there were slight nuances in workers' words about a child's young age across countries. Many participants in California thought that young children were "not able to understand" or articulate their wishes or were too vulnerable to be exposed to talking about maltreatment. Some of the Californian participants saw young children as important sources of information during the investigation of child maltreatment. A few of the Norwegian workers perceived young children as individuals who know what is going on in the family. None of the Norwegian workers depicted young children as vulnerable because of their young age. This is interesting given prior research findings: Skivenes (2015) compared Norwegian child protection workers' attitudes about a child's age when they assessed the risk to a child. Her study revealed that Norwegian child protection workers embraced a protective and paternalistic attitude towards children younger than 15 years, and a self-determination-focused attitude towards older children. The protective, paternalistic attitude was evident when Norwegian workers in my sample discussed imminent and high risk to a child as a non-participation trigger. This finding suggests that, to these Norwegian workers, the presence of serious risk might cancel out the principle of children's participation. The data material also showed that children's participation depends on the stage of the case. The words of the study participants working at the front end of cases (doing risk assessments in investigations) indicated that there is less participation during investigations than once children have been removed from home.

The frequency of responses of the two samples differed in terms of disability and mental illness. A smaller proportion of Norwegian workers discussed severe disability and mental health problems as reasons not to involve a child. It is difficult to explain this difference. It could be that Norwegian workers feel more confident in involving children with a disability or mental illness or the reverse, that disability and mental illness lie in their professional blind spot, and that workers in California might be more attuned to issues related to disability and mental illness. It could also be that the labels 'disability' and 'mental illness' are differently and perhaps more negatively interpreted in the US than in Norway. This finding needs further empirical exploration given the fact that children with a disability are more likely to suffer from child abuse and neglect (US Department of Health and Human Services. Administration for Children and Families. Administration on Children, Youth and Families, 2018b); that young people with disabilities are overrepresented in the child population in foster care in the US (Slayter, 2016), and that mental illness is prevalent among children in care in Norway and the US (Lehmann et al, 2013; Turney and Wildeman, 2016). According to Turney and Wildeman (2016, p 1), 'children in foster care are in poor mental and physical health relative to children in the general population, children across specific family types, and children in economically disadvantaged families'.

Study participants in both countries identified negative emotional impact as a non-participation trigger. This finding echoes a 2012 study of Norwegian child protection workers' attitudes by Vis et al, which showed that workers' protective attitudes, especially fear that involvement might harm children, constitute a barrier to children's participation (Vis et al, 2012). The fact that over three times as many Californian as Norwegian workers gave adverse emotional consequences for the child as a reason for not involving them suggests that the Californian participants may be more aware of the emotional consequences of involving children in their work. This might be due to the overrepresentation of emergency response workers in the Californian sample. These workers are probably more likely to meet children when they feel very distressed, so it is perhaps not surprising that emotional vulnerability was on the study participants' minds.

Study participants in both countries perceived imminent or high risk to the child as a non-participation trigger. This finding corroborates research showing that in emergency situations, when the risk to the child is serious and workers need to make decisions quickly to keep the child safe, child protection workers are more likely not to listen to children's opinions (Moldestad et al, 1998; van Bijleveld et al, 2014 Balsells et al, 2017). The findings about imminent risk were the mirror image to the findings on emotional vulnerability: over three times as many Norwegian participants mentioned immediate risk or the seriousness of abuse to the child as a reason for non-involvement. This might be partly a result of the character of the participant sample: the Californian study participants, many of whom were working in an emergency response unit, were more likely to encounter cases in which there was imminent risk to the child, and may have been more used to involving children in imminent risk situations.

Even if there was imminent risk, however, many Norwegian workers insisted that a child should be informed (but not necessarily make the decision). This finding makes sense when one considers how many of the Norwegian workers conceptualize 'involvement' as genuine participation, where a child influences the decision made: in decisions made in situations of imminent risk, these workers would not listen to the child's opinion but would proceed in a way they think keeps the child safe. The fact that there is a sizeable group of Norwegian workers in this sample who understand 'involvement' as genuine participation is supported by an analysis of a different interview question answered by the same sample of workers that Skivenes and Križ conducted in 2015 (Križ and Skivenes, 2015). This study analyzed the same workers' responses to the interview question, "What is your understanding of children's participation in child protection?". It found that a higher proportion of the Norwegian than Californian workers understood 'involvement' as genuine participation (Križ and Skivenes, 2015).

How could the law, policies and practice guidelines have influenced study participants' responses about reasons for non-involvement? The Norwegian study participants were more likely to conceive of younger children as knowledge-bearers who understood and could articulate what was happening in their families. It could be that this conceptualization of children reflects Norwegian child protection law (*Lov om Barneverntjenster*), which in 1992 established the right for children older than seven years to receive information and be heard (Vis et al, 2012; Berrick Duerr et al,, 2015b; Skivenes and Søvig, 2017). The law states that children younger than seven who can form their own opinion have the same right. The age participation threshold suggested by practice guidelines is higher in California. A 2010 document by the Californian Health and Human Services Agency that introduced TDMs in 11 counties mentioned the age of ten years as the participation threshold in TDMs about case plan development. One of the strategies discussed reads: 'Starting at age 10 involve and actively assist youth in identifying significant permanent persons and lost connections in the child's life with a goal of establishing legal permanency' (State of California Health and Human Services Agency, 2010, p 23). The Californian study participants' responses reflected the practice guidelines of the state of California about the reasons not to involve a child. This is how the 2017 guidelines draw the boundaries of participation around age and other parameters:

> When age-appropriate, a child or youth should always participate in a CFT [Child and Family Team] meeting. Participation should be limited if the nature of the meeting's agenda is not suitable for the child or youth. Some examples may include: the focus of the meeting is only about the parent or parents' needs, or the main topic of discussion is of a sensitive adult nature. There may also be times when a child or youth refuses to participate, or s/he does not feel comfortable attending. Further engagement of the child or youth may be needed to encourage their participation so that they have a voice within the team. Safety is another consideration for the team, as a child or youth may become easily angered or agitated during the CFT meeting and may require support. If applicable, the child or youth's mental health provider may also recommend if it is not in the

child or youth's best interest to attend the CFT meeting.
(Californian Department of Healthcare Services, 2017, p 6)

This chapter has showed that there are several factors in a child protection case that appear to prevent child protection caseworkers from involving children in genuine participation: a child's young age; severe disability or mental illness; potential negative impact of the child's participation on the child's emotional well-being; and imminent risk to the child. Further, the analysis of the interview material demonstrated that the study participants used different approaches to using information. Study participants said that they withheld information for fear of retraumatizing children further; they focused on gathering information during a child protection investigation, and they provided information to children at the front end of a case. These findings underline that children's participation varies depending on the stage in a child protection case and the child's age, ability, and level of vulnerability. They also reveal child protection caseworkers' attempts to straddle the tension between the protective and participatory ethos of child protection systems.

4

Participation triggers

This chapter examines which individual and contextual factors mattered to the study participants in situations when they heard children *and* took their statements or opinions and wishes seriously. These factors are called 'participation triggers' here. Sixty-seven workers (28 in Norway and 39 in California) were asked to describe a case in which a child's opinion mattered "a lot" to their decision-making. I analyzed the responses of workers who investigated reports of child abuse and neglect, and those who had provided or were providing ongoing services to children and families. The study participants could choose any situation they wanted to describe as the question was open-ended. In some cases, the participants were prompted to elaborate on what exactly it was that led them to believe that the child's opinion was significant in the case they were describing. That way I learned about the factors in actual cases.[1]

Three of the study participants, two in Norway and one in California, described situations that involved driving a car, metaphorically and/ or literally, either together as co-drivers with children or in a convoy. The participants' use of this imagery is revealing. Driving together suggests two things: first, both drivers can decide about the direction in which the vehicle is moving, a process that is facilitated by the co-drivers talking with each other about where they would like to head next, when to take a break, and so on. Second, it indicates that there are two individuals in the vehicle who are old enough and skilled enough to drive. The three examples of co-driving situations involved older teens and illustrated that "co-driving" (read: co-deciding) was affected by the child's age and ability to communicate their wishes clearly, convincingly and credibly. They also involved mutual trust and the worker's commitment to constant communication, which took effort and time. This finding resonates with one of the arguments in prior literature discussed in Chapter 2: a respectful relationship between children and caseworkers, established through information-giving and gathering, is a crucial building block towards children's genuine participation.

N11, one of the two Norwegian workers who used the co-driving image, mentioned a 17-year-old on her caseload who was acting out in her foster home and using drugs. The teen was supposed to be moved to another, more specialized, foster home while she was in drug treatment; however, she was adamant about not wanting to leave her current foster home. N11 recalled: "The girl prayed on her knees to get another chance. She didn't want to move from the foster home and stated that it was good for her." When asked what convinced N11 to heed the girl's opinion, N11 responded:

> 'I worked with her for some time because she was so convincing in her argumentation ... I was assured that she was in a foster home where they follow up, and we had an agreement that if that didn't work out, we would go for [the other] placement. So we drove that race together. She was convincing, and it's a kind of mutual trust.'

C2, an ongoing caseworker in California, used the image of driving when she recalled how the mutual trust built through communication allowed her to follow the lead of a 16-year-old. C2 described how she, literally and figuratively, became the teen's driver. The teen had been placed in foster care at the age of nine because she was physically abused by her mother, who was suffering from mental health issues and a substance use disorder. She had been in and out of foster homes since then and was living with an older sister at the time of the interview. When the case was assigned to C2, the teen mistrusted social workers. C2 managed to gradually gain her trust by telling her about her own history growing up in the city where they both lived. She explained to the teen that she was there to help, not to tell her what to do. At one point the teen explained her mistrust of social workers to C2:

> ' "Not you," she goes, "but all the other ones, they're old, and they come in here and it's all about telling me what to do". And she goes, "You know what? You haven't even said one thing about ... everything you're doing right now is you're just asking me questions, what I want, what I would like to do, what do I see [in my future], what are my plans? Not once have you ever said, "This is what you're going to do". And I looked at her. I'm like, "It's not my job to tell you what to do; it's my job to help you get what it is you want". And then after that, you know, she called me.'

In this situation C2 conceded control to the teen. When the teen overdosed on drugs while staying at her sister's house, she asked her sister to call C2 and tell her about it. C2 first took the teen out for lunch and discussed different programmes for her. Then she called a TDM meeting with the teen, her sister and others. When the teen did not speak up in the meeting, C2 told her, "Well, look, you know, I need you to talk. I need them to hear you the way I hear you." Then she continued to say, "and it takes a while". The teen called C2 after the meeting and told her that she wanted to move back into one of her former foster homes. C2 described what happened next:

> 'And, yeah, she actively went and looked for them. She actively went and advocated for herself to get into an independent programme at school. And all this because I didn't tell her what to do, you know? [laughs] … In that situation, she took responsibility for herself, and I was just, basically, I was just a car, you know. I just drove her where she needed to go.'

A little later in the interview, C2 stated: "And, yeah, it works better when they're teenagers because I don't think a seven-year-old would do that … My seven-year-old wanted a bed all to herself, which is what she got. This one here basically wanted to take [control], you know, she wanted to be in charge." In this situation the child protection worker and the child engaged in child-initiated participation. These two case descriptions show how children's age and ability to communicate their wishes clearly and convincingly and the trust between children and caseworkers affect the degree to which the workers attached significance to the child's opinion.

Table 4.1 shows the contexts of the cases mentioned by over 10 per cent of those study participants who recalled specific cases – 27 workers in Norway and 37 in California.

The percentage of the participants – a little over one third in total – who depicted a situation in which children wanted to move out of their current homes (either their parents' house or a foster home) to a new home was almost equal in Norway and California. The Californian workers were more likely to describe cases of physical and sexual abuse. This could be due to the fact that many of the study participants in California were recruited in emergency response units, where workers deal with assessing risk to the child during an investigation, whereas ongoing workers make decisions about the foster home and other services. In addition to the case contexts shown in Table 4.1, one worker in Norway and five workers in California discussed emotional abuse. Four workers in Norway discussed visitation schedules, but none

Table 4.1: Case contexts leading to participation, by frequency (n=64)

Contexts	Norway 100% (n=27) % (n)	US (California) 100% (n=37) % (n)	Total 100% (n=64) % (n)
Children's wish: move out of their parents' homes or foster home into a placement/new placement	37% (10)	35% (13)	36% (23)
Physical abuse	19% (5)	41% (15)	31% (20)
Choice of foster home	26% (7)	16% (6)	20% (13)
Parental substance abuse	26% (7)	14% (5)	19% (12)
Children's wish: stay in their parents' home or foster home or return to their parents' home	22% (6)	14% (5)	19% (11)
Parental conflict or domestic violence	19% (5)	8% (3)	12% (8)
Sexual abuse	0% (0)	22% (8)	12% (8)

Table 4.2: Participation triggers, by frequency (total n=67)

Factors	Norway 100% (n=28) % (n)	US (California) 100% (n=39) % (n)	Total 100% (n=67) % (n)
Children older than 12 years	68% (19)	61% (24)	64% (43)
Clear or credible communication	54% (15)	33% (13)	42% (28)
Corroborating evidence	29% (8)	44% (17)	37% (25)
Expression of fear, despair and sadness	36% (10)	38% (15)	37% (25)
Workers' positive perception of the child	14% (4)	26% (10)	21% (14)

of the Californian workers did. Only one worker in Norway and one worker in California discussed a case involving neglect.

As Table 4.2 shows, the most frequent factors leading to participation that emerged from the data were related to children's age and their ability to communicate their wishes clearly, persistently or credibly. The study participants mentioned children's expression of fear, the presence of evidence corroborating children's opinions or wishes, and the workers' positive attitude towards the child as factors promoting participation. I shall discuss these themes later.[2]

Children older than 12 years

Most of the situations that workers in both countries described in which children's opinion significantly mattered to their decision involved pre-teens or teens. The average ages discussed by the participants who mentioned children's specific ages were 12.6 years for Norway and 13 years for California. None of the participants mentioned a child younger than five and older than 16 years. Nineteen Norwegian participants and 24 Californian participants mentioned age in relation to decision-making. Only three of the Norwegian participants described a case of a child younger than ten years when talking about decision-making. One Norwegian participant mentioned a five-year-old, another one an eight-year-old child, and a third one mentioned a child between eight and nine years old. Three of the Californian participants discussed a child younger than ten: one referred to a six-year-old, one to a child between eight and nine, and another participant mentioned a nine-year-old child.

Several participants (12 out of 67) explicitly stated that age was a factor that affected the way in which they weighed children's opinions. These participants mentioned that the opinions of "older children" – understood as teens and less often pre-teens (ten- to 12-year-olds) – counted because they could articulate their opinions better than younger children. Teens, workers reasoned, would resist any decision made by the child protection agency that they did not agree with and could potentially put themselves at risk as a result. A few workers simply stated that it was young people's age that made them consider their opinion. N26 discussed a youth who was turning 15 and wanted to make her own decisions about her confirmation (a ceremonial rite of passage into her religious community). When asked why she contributed so much significance to the girl's opinion in that case, N26 responded: "It's because she's so big … it's obvious really that she should decide". N6 talked about the case of a 12-year-old youth who was in foster care and had visited his mother, who had suffered from an alcohol use disorder for years. The child protection agency sought to reduce the number of visitation meetings because they felt that the teen was being torn between the foster carer and the mother, but the child was fine with the same number of visits. N6 reflected on why the county board listened to the teen: "They listened to him, of course, because he was so big".

When asked to describe a situation in which she weighed the child's opinion heavily in her decision-making, C36 responded:

> 'Teens generally have a very, very loud voice, overall, about a lot of things, because ultimately, even though you might have parent–teen conflict, if a teen tells you they refuse to go back, they don't want to go back, they're fearful, or they're just plain downright mad [angry] and they don't want to go back, or they're just being difficult, whatever, we don't send the children back. So ... in those cases, those children have the highest, loudest voice that you definitely listen to.'

Several participants explained that older children can make their voice heard more clearly because they are able to communicate more effectively. They either express their wishes verbally or through actions – they run away, for example. Only one Norwegian worker, N16, mentioned older children's right to be heard as the reason why their opinion mattered to her: "I think that I'm very clear with everyone. When they're 15 years they have their own rights. They must be heard before that and, but [sic] their opinions must be taken into account." A few of the workers mentioned that teenagers would simply "vote with their feet" (C15) and run away if they were not happy with their current home, parents and foster parents. C35 mentioned how effectively a 16-year-old can influence the choice of foster placement:

> 'a lot of times in placement, if [it's] a child, we go to a TDM and the aunt says, "I'm right here, place the child with me", and the child is 16 and says, "I'm not going there. If you place me there, I'm going to run away". Well, I'm not going to place her there, so we need to know those things for the safety of the child.'

C15 stated:

> 'I think this is typically true when children are older. For example, even if there's like a safety concern, let's say that there's extensive parental substance abuse going on, or there might be domestic violence. Or physical abuse, so unless it is life threatening where we have no choice. If an older child refuses to be removed from the care of the parent, you know, we have to work, you know, with the child in terms of making the environment as safe as possible. That's one

of the considerations. Or we may have children who, as we say, vote with their feet. So children, they were removed from their parents and are put in foster care, and they're continuously running away from foster care, and running home to their parent. In those kinds of situations, we need to work with the child in keeping them safe in the home. It can also be the other way around … if a child discloses more about abuse in the home than we may have thought [when deciding] the child is safe to stay at home, and it's very clear that we [need to remove them].'

N13 discussed a case of two teens who she thought should have been removed from home but were not because they would have resisted the move. She explained, "But it's when they've become so big that even if we think the conditions are totally unsatisfactory where they are, they'd create so much resistance when being moved that it would only make matters worse". N12 explained that children's opinion counted when they were older and able to clearly express their wishes:

'[In] those situations where the children themselves … speak up. It's clear that she really wants that; if the child – these are maybe a bit older children who know how to put things into words and manage to actually walk up to a nurse or a teacher or someone like that – who in one way or the other then comes to us, and says that I have it so hard at home and explains it with pretty serious stuff, so it's clear that we must [act]. So the [child's] statement is very, very important.'

N28 recalled "a case where the child was in care, and this child was very resistant to being in care … But the child had very strong opinions about the placement and it had great impact. It was an older child."

Clear or credible communication

Many of the examples the study participants described focused on children and young people who articulated clearly or credibly how they were neglected or abused in their home and convincingly expressed their opinion and wishes. Participants used the adjectives "articulate" and "mature" to describe the children they were talking about, and they used the following terms to characterize their statements and expressions of opinion: clear, consistent, convincing, credible, detailed, honest, insistent, sensible, specific and persistent. Workers mostly referred to verbal communication, mentioning dialogue, conversations in meetings and "talking". In a few cases, workers described how children's non-verbal expressions made it clear what happened to the child in the home or what the child thought should happen.

The study participants who worked as investigators at the front end of cases mentioned situations in which children clearly and credibly communicated how they had been maltreated by their parents or caregivers. The credibility of verbal statements could be magnified by children displaying a certain affect when discussing what had happened to them. C4 stated:

'I think it's based on how well the child communicates and how honest they appear to be. And how affected they are by the situation. I've interviewed some children who've been profoundly affected by domestic violence in the way that they physically react, and the way that they talk about what's going on when they talk about the fighting and stuff.'

C1 discussed a case involving three siblings – a three-year-old, a nine-year-old and a 12-year-old – who were neglected by their mother. C1 decided to remove the children from home because the three-year-old, who was suffering from epilepsy, ran around in the neighbourhood without supervision, and "the older children who were able to speak did not want to return home [and] were very adamant. They showed a lot of emotional disturbance, flat affect, really anxious to get away from their home and felt very neglected by the mother". C1 described how the children's demeanour affected the extent to which she took the children's statements seriously:

'We were making a determination, and I felt that it warranted a closer look because this [mum] was a professional person and she was highly educated. It didn't make sense, so I knew there was more going on with the story. And it turns out there was a lot more going on with the story. So the children had an impact on that – their whole demeanour when I interviewed them – and I felt they were old enough to really have a rational thought and opinion about what was going to happen to them.'

N22 remembered an investigation of a physical abuse case involving a 15-year-old of immigrant background who reported that she was beaten by her parents and wanted to leave home. N22 explained why she took her opinion seriously:

'in investigative cases we like to gather information and try to create a decent picture ... of the situation, but in that case her words and her experience were enough in themselves. Whether it was because it was about violence, or it was because she herself managed to be so clear about what the problems were ... it was a combination of a lot.'

C6 explained the importance of credible communication by the child in sexual abuse cases:

'I think our sexual abuse cases are the biggest ones where the child ... what they're telling us matters and weighs in a lot. Because often in sexual abuse cases it's a matter of "he said, she said". There's often no evidence; there's no physical evidence. So there have been times when we've actually sent cases to court just based solely on what the child told us. And we found them credible and their story was consistent over time. Their body language matched what they were telling us. So there are times when we take that into account 100 per cent.'

N27 discussed the case of an eight-year-old-girl whose case was reported to the child welfare agency by the school. Her description of abuse struck N27 as credible and sincere:

'We got statements from the school about what the eight-year-old had said there at school. The school then contacted us. We get to hear that the child ... is credible in a way. We talk with the child herself and experience the same. We find that the child only, indeed, expanded in a way what she'd previously said. Didn't go back to any stories or came with other things into the story. We find that the child is serious when it was said. Yes, and ... she stuck by ... the story, or stories, and ... it was a child who didn't want to move away from her parents, but who somehow stuck by her story anyway. So I think that ... here it was very important to take the child seriously. And what we think is common, is that children pull back these kinds of stories ... but that didn't happen here ... we experienced the child as a child who was sincere.'

The experience of C29 illustrates that it is important to the worker's decision that the child clearly communicates their situation: the study participant worked with a 16-year-old LGBTQ youth whose parents had immigrated to the US from Latin America. He was trying to come out to his parents, but they did not accept his sexuality. C29 said that she was struck by the teen's honesty and specificity about the consequences of his problems at home. She continued:

'So that was a difficult experience, because there was no physical abuse from the parents, no evidence of strong emotional abuse, you know; the fact that these parents come from a different country to the US, the fact that this child came at young age to the US and has acculturated, makes him be sort of in-between. And now he has these issues and doesn't know which way to go. I don't know. I could sense that he was suffering a lot emotionally. So, he was very convincing. And I asked him, "How do you want me to help you? What do you think you need?" So, we worked together on a plan. And eventually the child chose to be out of home.'

C39 recalled a situation involving a 15-year-old whose family was from the Middle East. The teen had called the child protection agency because her parents threatened to send her back to their country of origin to get married. She was staying out with male friends after school and did not come home on time. C39 explained that she put significant weight on the teen's statements "because her behaviour was so extreme ... What ended up happening was she escaped from the home; she jumped out the front window and ran to a neighbour's house, and the neighbours called us."

N19 discussed an investigation involving a five-year-old boy who did not speak but clearly expressed the abuse he had experienced in a non-verbal manner:

'In an investigation, there was actually a child who didn't speak, and he showed me, he was five years old and didn't speak. He came up to me and I asked the mother about the child's father, if he had ever touched the child or hit him. And then the mother said that he had not. And the child came up to me and managed to express that dad took his arm and twisted it. It was a very crucial factor in how I kept on working in the family.'

N28 recounted the following example to illustrate that children do not always express their wishes verbally:

'But it's quite strong when a child, for example, on a trip with a case manager goes through a tunnel and says, "Can we not drive to Crystal Beach? I've never been on Crystal Beach". And the child is ten years old and has lived in the town for her entire life and the family has a car ... Then it will be, I think, quite clear statements like that in relation to what children need, without the child saying that I wish for that or I want that; then it becomes so clear.'

The study participants talked about situations when children clearly stated that they did not want to stay with their family. N2 told us about a case involving children who were 11 and 12 years old and living with their mother who used alcohol and drugs and neglected the children's needs. N2 stated that the children "were incredibly clear that they didn't want to live there", and, a few moments later in the interview, she repeated, "The kids were so clear on that one; they just didn't want to stay there". Using similar wording, C18 discussed a case in which two teenagers had moved out of the home, where their mother had emotionally abused them, and moved in with their older sister. The teens did not want to return to their mother when the sister moved to another part of the country. This is how C18, who said that she "really felt particularly engaged with the kids", described the situation: "they really wanted – they did not feel comfortable going home. They were very articulate; they came across as very believable and very mature for the most part, and I just wasn't going to have that happen."

N16 recalled "situations at home when I don't think I'd have gone to the county board [and recommended removal], but the child expressed such a strong wish to get away from her mother, for example, that I went comparatively far to find other solutions". N16 conceded that she does not always weigh children's opinion even when they're very clear about what they want: "It was also where children were very clear that they don't want to live where they're living, or they're placed in an institution, and I decided not to move them, because I believed it was the best for them, and they continued to be where they were;

that they needed time". In this case, the child's clear articulation of their wishes was balanced out by N16's assessment of what was in the best interests of the child.

Other participants discussed putting significant weight on children's opinion in situations where decisions were made about parental visits and foster placements. The study participants considered children's wishes if they were articulate about what they wanted. N26 discussed the case of a 14-year-old who tried to schedule visits by her mother in the way she wanted. N26 considered the teen's opinion significant because "the girl was very good at expressing herself; very clever in saying what she thinks and believes. She thinks about things, and the mother makes her very uneasy". C3 mentioned a 14-year-old who was placed in a group home and did not want to move to a foster home: "He really is too young to be in [a residential home], but he was adamant he didn't want to live in a foster home; he wanted to continue in the group home because he wanted to go home [to his parents], and he didn't want another family". N18 discussed the case of a 13-year-old whose parents had agreed to a voluntary placement in a residential home, but the girl wanted to stay with her father. N18 explained what it was that made her consider the youth's opinion important: "It was because she was a very mature girl. She was very clear about what she wanted. And I thought that such a move against her will, it … would be worse for her in the long term."

Corroborating evidence of abuse

When the study participants discussed situations in which a child's opinions, wishes and statements were significant to their decision, many of them mentioned additional evidence that supported what the child was saying or what the child wanted to happen. One of the Norwegian workers used the verb "triangulate" when referring to the process of supporting the child's evidence of abuse with the help of other data points. (In this case it was the statement of the school principal, who knew the children well, that the investigating worker used as corroborating evidence to triangulate the children's statements.) Corroborating evidence could consist of: physical evidence, such as bruises on a child's body, that substantiated children's statements about parental abuse (in an investigation); the statements of other professionals who interacted with the children; or workers' observations of child-parent or child-caregiver interactions in the home or in meetings. Evidence from previous interactions with the family was seen as evidence, too, if the family had a history with the child protection agency. A few of the participants mentioned evidence in the context of cases where the children's statements were the only evidence they had to go on. This was especially evident in cases of child sexual abuse; when talking about these cases, several workers stated that children's statements mattered a lot to them in these cases, even if there were no other evidence supporting them.

There were other examples of this. C36 mentioned "abuse cases, where you've got the child telling you, [and] you've also got the physical evidence of what's going on". C5 said, "if it's physical abuse, if … their [children's] stories match the wounds". C11 explained the criteria that render a child's statement significant to her decision: "[with] children, in physical abuse cases … the ability to tell me that this is a one-time thing versus something that happens consistently, which will either match with the marks or not match with the marks". C15 stated: "There was one particular case where there was abuse to a 15-year-old child, and it was important not only to see the abuse, but to have the child describe to me what the abuse was like, and it matched everything I saw visually". C8 responded by mentioning a child's display of fear, coupled with physical evidence of abuse and her own observation of the parents verbally abusing the child when she was interviewing the child:

> 'If a child says that they're afraid to go home, I'm going to honour that. I know that my investigation is not complete until I speak to a parent, but if the child is covered with bruises and they tell me that they're afraid to go home, I'm going to listen. That's going to speak loudly to me. If when the parent gets there, they are very remorseful and the child curls up in their lap, I'm going to see that that was perhaps a temporary fear about going home. But you still have to deal with that feeling. It didn't just instantly go away. So that's a very big factor for me; and then you might have a parent who comes in and screams at the child, at which point I would probably ask for the police to remove the child because, in fact, if the child's afraid to go home, I would want to honour that and give the child a little space until the child did feel safe. So that to me, that's the biggest thing with children … Now with a sexually abused child, I'm very conservative and so … I'd rather err on the side of safety and get the child out of the home or the perpetrator out of the home if the parent can be supportive … But anyway, that's probably the biggest factor for me.'

C34 recalled the case of a teenager who said she did not want to go home because her parents hit her. The teen did not want to speak in the meeting about the case, but she spoke to a support person afterwards and told her that "the allegations are false". C34 discussed the saliency of hearing corroborating evidence by other people who are familiar with the youth. Then she continued: "And so it's crucial at every aspect to hear what the child has to say, but at the same time try to gather as much information from other people that know, not only the family [but also] the child … to make it stronger, the case, if the allegations are actually true". N27 mentioned a situation that illustrates the importance of evidence supporting a child's statement of abuse:

> 'I've got a case now where [it's] the child's statements – and it is only the child's statements, there's no other evidence, let's put it like that – that has caused that we've decided that the child should then not stay at home. Where the child says they're being beaten, and there are no others who say that it [happened], but the child said it. The child is eight years and stands by it. The adults around say that the child has a somewhat lively imagination. And it's a matter now that went to the county board, where we then hear that, we have no evidence, we have only the child's statements.'

N27 said that the parents' lawyer contested the child's statement, but the tribunal took her seriously because of evidence from school staff who backed up the child.

The following quotes evidence the importance of the worker's observations of children's interactions with their caregivers: C30's observations of the meetings with a boy on her caseload were evidence corroborating the boy's wishes when she was deciding about where to place the boy:

> 'I was in meetings with him on several occasions to assess, with him and with mum. We were trying to place him back with mum, or with a relative, with grandma, or auntie. I was just watching the interaction between the mum and the child. They were not getting along. I could see mum had a lot of issues on her own. Mental health issues and being very in-your-face with that child. I could see why it was so difficult for him to be there. Mum was just like, "I can't take this anymore. I don't want to deal with him." The child's like, "I don't want to be here with you, either".'

C18 described a similar dynamic when she was working with two teenage girls whose "mum had a history of many different referrals, and these kids had been in foster care before". C18 talked about a TDM, "where the mum really showed her true colours about just her inability to interact with these kids in a positive way, and so like, wow, okay, [not having the girls live with mum] is the right thing to do". N20 said that she moved a child from a foster home because of the reactions of the foster parents in a meeting. The child "did say that he wanted to move and there was a lot of conflict, but he was essentially moved because the foster parents didn't say anything [positive], there was nothing positive they could say about him; not even that he had beautiful eyes or anything". C14 recalled a similar situation when she was in the process of moving a 14-year-old into a foster home after the teen had been removed from home. C14 decided not to place him with the foster family she had in mind based on the teen's perceptions and her impression of the foster parents:

> 'And I got the child to the home, and we went in, and we met with the foster parents and started talking, and they reacted to this kid in some ways that really bothered me. Like, "You're going to have to behave here. And we don't put up with any … I'm the dad, and she's the mum, and we've got a good house here" … there was just things that were being said, but … it was like five o'clock on Friday night, and so I went to leave and this kid said to the foster parents, "I'm going to walk my social worker to her car". And we went out to the car and he said, "[Name of worker], please don't leave me here; these people don't like me. I could tell off the bat, they don't like me. Please don't leave me here tonight." And I said, "OK". And I went back in, and I said, "There's been a change, and we're not going to be leaving him here tonight with you, we're going to find another place for him to be". I went back and … made arrangements for him to stay with his grandfather, who he was OK with on a temporary basis. And then the next week we started looking at what the alternatives were.'

Expression and display of fear, despair and sadness

More than one third of the study participants mentioned that a child's verbal and/or non-verbal display of negative affect – including fear, depression, despair, distress, sadness and weariness – influenced their decision-making. The Norwegian workers mentioned children who displayed desperation or weariness of the situation they found themselves in, and who expressed that they "had it so hard" at home. The majority of the Californian study participants who discussed children's expression of emotions talked about distress or fear. None of the Norwegian participants mentioned a display of fear as a significant factor. The following quotes provide evidence of the role a child's expression of fear, desperation, distress, sorrow and weariness play in decision-making.

N16 explained that a child's opinion mattered much in situations when the child was desperate:

> 'It's because I experience the child being so desperate. We're in a situation where the child is at the limit of what is justifiable. And then I think the child is on the verge of failing further in one way or the other; failing to succeed, which makes it so they cannot stay where they're living.'

N15 described a case where the child's wish to move into a foster home was influenced by the child's verbal communication of their despair:

N15: 'The final nail in the coffin, one can put it that way ... [is] when the child ... [has] had enough, cannot bear it anymore, doesn't want to continue. It's clear, there are quite strong words that don't come so often. It often comes on top of everything else we worry about and think about. It's clear that, it becomes enough to speed up the process.'

Interviewer: 'If the child says clearly, "I want to move".'

N15: 'Yes, when it's enough, in a way. They rarely say those exact words, but "I can't bear it anymore", and then in the conversation, when we, because I experience often that children are [prepared] and look forward [to us coming] and [say], "I've been waiting for you the whole week, you didn't come before [name of day]", [they're] ready, [ready to be] moving. The kids, they've had enough sometimes. It's a relief when someone says that [they must move]; it's a relief mixed with great sorrow, but there and then, that someone says, no, now you must move. But other things ... children can be quite clear that they wish that mum yells less, for example, that she's not so angry, and so on. And it can greatly help determine the type of intervention measure. Or, not only in itself, but it has an influence.'

N23 described the case of a 16-year-old who had been removed from home because of his mother's substance use disorder. He wanted to return to his mother, who had started rehabilitation. "He's now lived with his mother for almost a year, has a job, is in therapy, and he's very happy that he lives with his mum". N23 alluded to the fact that the teen had suffered from depression because he had been separated from his mother: "The negative development has certainly stopped and perhaps it was reversed. And this is a boy who's much happier. I was also a little worried about his psyche. He seemed ... to be quite heavy of mind in any case. And it seems that has disappeared. He's in a much better disposition." N4 discussed the case of a teenage girl who had troubles with her family for a long time and ran away from home. She had been gone for a week before the police found her. N4 delineated the situation: "And then she came here with her dad, and then both the girl and the father indicated that they're weary somehow; totally tired of the situation now, not moving forward".

N21 discussed the case of a 12-year-old who told the child welfare agency that she did not want to live at home anymore. The agency had tried several intervention measures but to no avail. The agency then placed her in a foster home. N21 reflected on the case: "We'd been thinking that she should move, but it happened much sooner because she came and said it herself, when she was 12". When the participant was asked what it was about the girl's expression or opinion that rendered it important, N21 replied, "because it was credible, and because we'd also gotten it from others ... it was not just a girl who was angry at the parents. It was a girl who had it really hard and was little cared for." C14 used similar words to describe the case of a teen whom she removed from a relative's home: "And he's had a really hard life ... and he was like, I can't do it. If I have to stay there, I can't say what's going to happen. And he was removed from that situation and put into foster care."

The following quotes demonstrate the importance of children's display of distress or fear in workers' decision to remove a child from home in the context of emotional, physical or sexual abuse. C28 said that she would heavily weigh a child's opinion in the case of "a child voicing fear, a child voicing that he or she is afraid to go home. A child voicing that there's ongoing beatings, a child voicing that he or she's afraid and that mum has not protected her from molestation by Uncle Charlie."

C27 stated that a child's expression of distress affected her decision:

'If I see that it's causing a child considerable distress in what they're telling me, I definitely take that as far as a decision-making impact or as something that I'm very concerned about. And their distress may be in their observations, in the language they're using, the event they're telling, gauging for whether they've harmed themselves, what kind of situations they're putting themselves in.'

C26 recalled the following situation:

'There's a case where the child disclosed to me that they were fearful to go home, because they had just disclosed that their father beats them with a belt and had told them not to disclose anything ... And they ended up telling the school, and therefore [the school] told me when I went to go interview that child, and [so] I wasn't about to let that child go back home. I had to make other arrangements, place with an extended family member, and the courts got involved. And that was strictly based on the interview with the child.'

C40 remembered a case involving a 12-year-old:

'I had a case, not too long ago, the boy was 12, so he was older, but we had a TDM, and he wanted to participate. I asked him and I said, "Come on in here", and his father was very depressed and physically abusive, and the child told me he had been hit with a [coat]hanger, and he did have a mark ... he said that he didn't like that and he felt that he needed to be away from his father because his father was very abusive to him. And that child's opinion mattered a lot to me because he said, "I can't talk to my father for fear of having repercussions". So, I really wanted to give him voice, so he came in the TDM and what he said was so brilliant.'

Workers' positive perceptions of the child

When study participants had positive perceptions of a child, such as "a good student" and/or a "nice kid", the child appeared to be more deserving of participation in the worker's mind than when the worker perceived the child negatively. (Negative views of teens will be described in Chapter 6.) C10's story is a good illustration of how positive perception may affect the extent to which a child's statements matter in the worker's decision. C10 described the case of a 15-year-old who stated that his parents physically and emotionally abused him by hitting him and calling him names. C10 explained why she decided to believe the boy:

> 'I did weigh it a lot for him because to me, I mean, I've dealt with a lot of out-of-control teens, they make up stories, but this one, I did not feel the same. And then, I also talked to other professionals because the parents are the ones that were saying that he was lying. But the principal said, "No, he's a good kid" and the grandparents said that "No, I witnessed the verbal abuse". So, I did put a lot of weight on what he told me. I pretty much told the parents that this is what he told me, this is what I got, and you guys have to back off from that because the parents probably are saying that he's lying.'

Another example of a positive view of the child was provided by C18, who described a case involving two teenage girls whose mother was emotionally abusive to them. C18 described the girls as "terrific kids and doing well in school and very involved in the school". She listened to the girls' wish and removed them from home. C24's quote shows that a worker categorizing a child as "a good kid" results in the worker listening to the child. C24 recounted saying in a conversation with a teenager, "You're a good kid; I see your grades; I listen to what you said".

C14 talked about an LGBTQ teen who lived in the same home with his mother, who was addicted to pain medication. As the teen was coming out, his mother reacted very violently, and the teen ended up moving into a friend's mother's home. C14's quote illustrates the importance of positive perceptions:

> 'And he was able to be who he needed to be in a safe, loving environment. And so I think, for that, because of the mum's just really hurtful language, and just the way she dealt with him, it was just a really sad situation. Very emotionally abusive and very physically abusive. And he was the nicest kid ever; I mean, just the sweetest kid. So, for him, that was huge. Just his emotion around it, and his sort of desperation.

Like, I was really worried, if he stayed in that environment, he would try to kill himself. It was that bad.'

Two Norwegian workers, N2 and N20, described the children whose cases they discussed as "tough". One referred to children who were courageous and strong enough to call their mother out on her lies in front of the worker: "So those kids say 'That's a lie, mum'. I think they were so tough. Mmm. Courageous." N20, the worker who worked on the case previously mentioned with the 16-year-old whose foster parents had nothing positive to say about him and who wanted to change foster homes, also described the teen as "tough". The worker decided to move him into another foster home but ran into an obstacle – a lack of foster homes. She elucidated: "There are not so many [foster homes] ... You do not get tough 16-year-olds into foster care, then, just like that. From one foster home to another. There aren't so many in line so that ... it's not always that we can do what we believe is right."

Two Norwegian study participants implied that they trusted children and felt they were truthful. N7 discussed the case of a 14-year-old of immigrant background who contacted the child welfare agency with the help of the school nurse because she felt pressured by her parents to consent to an engagement with her cousin, which she did not want. She had worked with the school nurse for a while but then the situation became untenable for her. Her parents threatened suicide to convince her that the her refusal would ruin the family's reputation. This is what happened:

'In that situation, the child was then placed outside the home – basically at a secret address – based on the story that she herself had told us. The decision was communicated to the parents after she was placed. The same day, but a few hours later. That one ended well. Many long conversations, meetings with the parents who went from [talking about] a quick ceremony to resisting our work to cooperating. The girl lives at home now and it works most of the time that they speak with her in a straightforward way. But it was her story alone that was crucial for the decision. And it was a pretty serious decision. We placed her at a secret address without talking with her parents about what she'd told us. We couldn't take the chance that she lied. If she's telling the truth, then it's serious. If she's lying ... but why should she be lying about that? We couldn't take the chance; we had to protect her. There were huge consequences, both for her and her family.'

N27 told us how she trusted an eight-year-old's statements about a case involving physical abuse based on guidance documents from the child welfare agency. The documents used research evidence showing that children do not fabricate stories about being physically or sexually abused:

> 'But we experienced the child as a child who was sincere, and ... we actually have now quite a few guidance documents on it in relation to violence, where the research says the fact is that children do not make up stuff like that. So, it's not common for children to invent violence stories or, for example, [stories of] sexual abuse. They'll rather try to hide [it] so that there won't be problems as a result of it or [so] the child [does] not feel guilty.'

Conclusion

The aim of this chapter was to tease out the case conditions that lead a child protection caseworker to take children's statements, opinions and wishes seriously. The study participants talked about situations involving collaboration between children and workers and child-led participation when they described the case scenarios where children's opinions counted. There were several common themes. Children's age mattered to the extent to which workers took their opinion seriously: most study participants described case examples that involved pre-teens and teens. This echoes previous research findings that demonstrated that age is an important factor in participation in risk assessment, care order hearings and case planning (Shemmings, 2000; Fox and Berrick Duerr, 2006; Vis and Thomas, 2009; Berrick Duerr et al, 2015a; Magnussen and Skivenes, 2015; Skivenes, 2015; Paulsen, 2015, 2016; Križ and Roundtree-Swain, 2017; Balsells et al, 2017).

Case context mattered: more than one third of the participants described situations that involved a child who wanted to be removed from their home, and the workers then ended up supporting the child's wish. In many of these cases, the child's expression of their experience or opinion was one piece of the evidence that workers were considering in the case. Several workers reported gathering evidence from other sources, such as teachers or the child's friends, as well. Many participants (in both countries) stated that they listened to children's opinion in situations when the evidence on the case corroborated what the children were saying or expressed that they wanted. Similarly, only a few of the study participants mentioned situations where the child protection agency wanted to remove the child, the child opposed that decision and the worker then supported the child and the child continued to live at home. This finding is in agreement with prior research, which showed that children's opinions were less likely to be heeded in situations where the child was considered at serious risk of harm (Moldestad et al, 1998; Vis et al, 2011; van Bijleveld et al, 2014. It corresponds with the findings of the study by Vis and Thomas (2009), which showed that children were more likely to participate when they were referred to the agency for reasons other than abuse and neglect.

The Norwegian study participants were more likely to discuss a child's opinion about visits with a parent or parents and children's and young people's choice of foster home. None of the participants in California discussed visits. The Californian participants focused on sexual, emotional, and physical abuse when they discussed situations in which a child's opinion was significant to their decision. Norwegian workers focused on parental substance use issues (drugs and alcohol). This did not seem to be down to a higher prevalence of drug and alcohol use in Norway: both drug use and alcohol consumption are higher in the US. The *World Drug Report* showed that the annual percentage of the population aged 15–64 years which consumes opioids in Norway amounts to 0.3, while it is an estimated 5.9 in the US (United Nations Office on Drugs and Crime, 2011). Cocaine, cannabis, and alcohol use is higher in the US than in Norway. On average, Norwegians older than 15 years consumed 6.1 litres of pure alcohol per person in 2014, while individuals in the US consumed 8.8 litres per person (OECD, 2017). It is likely that the Californian sample was more focused on child abuse because there were more emergency response workers in the Californian sample. These workers investigate child maltreatment, determine whether abuse has occurred, and assess how high the risk is to the child. The difference could also be due to differences in views on risk: the risk threshold is higher in the US than in Norway (Križ and Skivenes, 2013; Skivenes and Stenberg, 2015). In the US, the reports that get screened in for response and the cases that workers tend to deal with are more likely to be abuse cases in which the child is at imminent risk of harm. It could be that the problem perceptions of the study participants may be different in the two samples because of systemic differences in orientations to protecting children: Californian participants described abuse and neglect, Norwegian workers perceived parents' behaviour leading to the abuse and neglect as a problem. (A few of the Norwegian workers expressed negative views of parents with an alcohol and drug use disorder.) This reflects the family-service orientation of the Norwegian child protection system (Skivenes, 2011). Gilbert et al (2011) described the differences in systemic orientations like this:

> there also continues to be important differences among the countries [that the researchers studied, which included Norway and the US] in which child welfare systems respond to child abuse and neglect. For example, although child abuse and neglect continue to be the main organizing categories for child welfare work in the US and Canada, this is not the case elsewhere. (Gilbert et al, 2011, p 251)

The way in which children acted in the presence of the study participants – their manners of speaking, the words they used and their facial and bodily displays – appeared to matter to the degree to which the workers weighed children's opinions. The participants described children whose opinion counted as articulate, convincing, credible, honest, insistent, mature, or exhausted, desperate, fearful, and sad.

The symbolic-interactionist theory of Erving Goffman is useful in interpreting this finding, especially Goffman's view of social reality as enacted between individuals (Collins and Makowsky, 2009). Goffman (1959) viewed social life as a play in a theatre where individuals act out reality as if on stage. People (consciously or subconsciously) undertake 'impression management' to control situations and turn them in their favour. Children's impression management – the way in which they acted – affected the degree to which many of the study participants weighed their wishes and opinions.

In both countries, workers seemed to be more likely to take children's accounts and opinions seriously when they had positive perceptions of youth. This suggests that workers construct some young people (but not others) as worthy of participation by drawing symbolic boundaries. In doing so, they draw on the cultural registers that are available to them. The work of James et al (2008) is useful in interpreting this finding: the authors draw on anthropologist Mary Douglas's (1966) work to argue that symbolic boundary drawing is an important step in the process of producing citizenship. I shall weave this analytical thread further in Chapter 6, which analyzes in more detail how workers create symbolic boundaries between the youths they consider worthy and unworthy of participation.

5

Doing participation

This chapter analyzes when and how child protection caseworkers reported doing participation in their everyday practice. The term 'doing participation' refers to the range of possible participation, from minimal participation by listening to a child's opinions and reflections without taking them into consideration to promoting genuine participation in decision-making. The chapter examines to what degree the study participants facilitated genuine participation, defined as children's opinions being heard and weighed in decision-making. The decisions study participants discussed included the removal of children from home, support services, foster care placements and children's contact with their parent(s) while in care. The data for this chapter rest on the responses to the following interview questions answered by 28 child protection workers in Norway (N) and 40 workers in California (C). The first question was: "At what stage in a case do you involve children?" This question was often followed up by, "How do you involve children?" and "If your opinion differed from what should happen in a case with that of the child, how do you proceed?" The first two questions yielded information about what workers said they did when they involved children in the child protection cases they typically worked on. The third question provided data on the kinds of decisions in which they tended to disagree with children. It offered evidence on how workers weighed a child's opinion in a situation in which the child disagreed with them.

I used definitions of participation by Shier (2001), Thomas (2002) and Lansdown (2010) to assess the levels of children's participation that workers reported promoting. One of the bricks in Thomas's (2002) 'climbing wall' of participation is the support the child experiences in expressing their opinions and wishes. Another is the voice of the child in decision-making (Thomas, 2002). These are the five levels of empowerment distinguished by Shier: '1. Children are listened to. 2. Children are supported in expressing their views. 3. Children's views are taken into account. 4. Children are involved in decision-making processes. 5. Children share power and responsibility for decision-making' (Shier, 2001, p 110). Lansdown differentiates between three types of participation: 'consultative participation', 'collaborative

Table 5.1: Participatory approaches by frequency in total sample (n=68)

Themes	Norway 100% (n=28) % (n)	US (California) 100% (n=40) % (n)	Total 100% (n=68) % (n)
Giving information	61% (17)	60% (24)	60% (41)
Facilitating participation	39% (11)	50% (20)	46% (31)
Gathering information	25% (7)	57% (23)	44% (30)

participation', and 'child-led participation' – related to Shier's level five (Lansdown, 2010).

Table 5.1 shows that there are three ways in which the study participants reported doing participation: giving information, facilitating participation, and gathering information. Almost half of the total sample reported facilitating children's genuine participation. The kind of genuine participation that participants encouraged was primarily consultative. They asked children about their opinions and wishes and weighed them in decision-making. Only rarely did they collaborate with children on decisions or agreed to a decision that was child-initiated.

Giving information: the study participants reported involving children by providing them with information about the child protection process, workers' and the agency's roles and responsibilities, the process of meetings, and the availability of spokespersons. They provided logistical information about what happens during the child welfare process and informed children about who makes the decisions. They explained which decision they or the child protection agency had made, and why they had made that decision. When their opinion or decision contradicted any wishes children had volunteered, workers explained the rationale behind their decision(s) or the benefits of an intervention. It was evident that it took participants' time, patience and energy to provide information to children about the child protection process and the rationale behind their decisions. The participants also reported providing "emotional information" to children by signalling empathy, respect, and recognition.

Facilitating participation: this is the approach used by those participants who consulted children *and* gave them the opportunity to develop and express their own opinions and wishes. These workers showed interest in and respect for children's experiences and opinions by acknowledging their feelings and views. They signalled to children that they had heard and understood what they were saying. Workers tried to address children's feelings (of fear for parents, fear of parents, or guilt and loyalty to parents) and discussed their opinions with the children, even if, ultimately, children's opinions did not drive decision-making. Many of these participants mentioned situations where they decided against children's wishes because they believed the decision would not be in children's best interests. Participants were primarily concerned about children's safety, for example, if children wished to remain with a substance-abusing parent. Some of the participants facilitated participation by reassuring children that they would be heard in meetings. They informed children that they were entitled to be represented by a spokesperson (in Norway).

Gathering information: the answers of a quarter of the study participants in Norway and over half of the study participants in California showed that they primarily approached children as sources of information they needed during a child protection investigation so they could assess the risk to the child and the child's needs. The purpose of these workers' focus on evidence gathering was to keep the child safe. This approach was most prominent in the responses of those participants who conducted risk assessments at the front end of child protection cases – the emergency response workers interviewed in California and the workers investigating reports of abuse and neglect in Norway. These participants typically discussed how they involved a child when deciding whether the child was at imminent risk of harm and needed to be placed out of home. Their involvement of children consisted of asking questions and listening to them with the purpose of gathering evidence during the investigation.[1]

The participants reported employing only one of these approaches or two or all at the same time, depending on their responsibility in the agency (investigative versus ongoing child protection worker – who reviews a family's case and develops case plans for the family) and the case context, especially the severity of the case and the perceived level of risk to the child. Investigating workers focused on gathering information rather than providing it or facilitating participation (regardless of the country they practised in). When workers perceived an imminent risk to the child, they were more likely to gather and provide information than consult a child about their opinion. Not all the investigating workers mentioned involving children solely through gathering evidence. While this was the primary approach they were taking during an investigation, many stated that they provided information to children to inform them of what was happening and explained why they had made the decision they had made. In the subsequent sections, I shall discuss the three types of involvement in turn, starting with the most frequently mentioned approach in the sample overall – giving information.

Giving information

This is how C4 explained her role and responsibilities:

> 'I pretty much explain to [children] who I am, what my job is, and I usually say I'm a social worker, and I ask them if they know what that is. Some of them do, some of them don't. And I say, "We make sure that kids are safe, and … I'm just here to check in on you and see how you're doing".'

C1 discussed how she involved children in the initial interview by explaining her role and the investigation process:

> 'I tell them what's happening, why we're there. I allow them to ask questions. I try and make sure they understand; that they don't feel that something is being done to them, with them, [which would] create more fear and trauma … They deserve to understand that the idea is that they're going to be safe, and [someone will] check in with them. The children can call you if they want to call you sometimes. You're like their touchstone.'

C35 described placement choices: "We'd like the child to be aware of what the placement choices are and what we expect out of them". The participants said that they explained the decision-making process to children. N6 stated: "[we tell them] it's the county board who will ultimately decide. We believe that the child can't live at home, but the county board will decide it. And then we'll explain a little about foster care."

Several participants mentioned that they provided information about the rationale driving their decisions when they disagreed with the child. This is how C3 explained how she involved children in cases where she disagreed with their opinion: "just possibly explaining why things are the way they are, and why they have to be … Just a lot of explaining and a lot of trying to get them to really understand." The information and explanations workers provided were often couched in terms of the child's safety in words that workers thought children understood. C15, an emergency response worker, stated, "We don't ask a child about their opinion", but then continued to qualify her statement:

> 'But for example, if a child is older, and let's say we need to remove a child, we explain it to the child why they need to

be removed; why we think it's not safe for them at home. And we try to explain that in children's terms; that we don't think their mum or dad can take care of them right now or can keep them safe right now.'

C27 explained that in cases where she disagreed with the child:

'I'm usually going to let them know what the next action is I'm going to take in order to ensure their health and/ or their safety, and [that] apparently, we disagree on that. And I also let them know that they have a right to their opinion. And I try to articulate in a very simple manner what my opinion is.'

She then clarified with an example: "So I usually let them know, 'I'm worried about you getting hit by your mother again when she's drunk, and I'm just not comfortable with you staying there with her right now. So right now, maybe you should stay with your grandma for a couple of nights until we figure this out'." This is how N12 explained to a boy who was in foster care why he could not stay overnight at his father's house during parental visitation time:

'And then I must explain and say that I know that dad has [problems with drug use], and this boy knows it very well. Dad uses drugs, and this is why the child welfare service thinks it's unsafe [for the boy to stay there overnight], and I know that he hasn't always managed to take care of you like we want. And that there were some times when he was out of the house, for example on the night when you stayed there overnight. It happened before, and we know that dad is still using drugs. And then we cannot let you do it [allow you to stay overnight]. It becomes sort of like an explanation, trying to elaborate on what it is that makes the child welfare service think something different from him, because we thought it was best for him.'

Several workers in Norway explained to children that their views would be heard through a spokesperson. When N15 was asked what she would do if the child welfare agency planned a decision that the child opposed, she replied:

> 'I listen to that and convey that I realize that they, that is, I try to show that I understand their experience ... but we still want someone else to come in and help us to evaluate it, whether that is right. And that they will be heard. They get their own spokesperson, that is, all those things, so that we're absolutely confident that those who ultimately decide know 100 per cent what you want. But I explain anyway why I think that.'

N25's approach was very similar. She reassured the child that their opinion would be heard. This is how she responded to the question about differences in opinion:

> 'Then we'll need to talk with the child and tell them. In fact, it's not so long ago that it was I myself who had to tell the child that we in the child welfare agency believe that she cannot stay at home, and then she began to cry, and I told her that I see that you think that this is bad and that you are very fond of your mum, but this is what we're going to do anyway. But then I explained it very thoroughly, about the county board, that it is not we who decide, but that it is the county board who decides. That she will also be heard. I explained to her about this spokesperson who would come and stuff.'

C32 expressed that conversations with children whose opinion differed from hers were sometimes challenging: "If I disagreed, I would try to explain why I disagreed and ... why we needed to do it my way, or why what they wanted to do wasn't going to work for them or ... their siblings or whatever it was that they wanted. That often doesn't work out very well, particularly with teenagers". The following quote by C35 illustrates the challenges of these kinds of conversations:

> 'We have a child who has to go to a residential treatment centre. The child has some real major problems. Well, of course, the child is seven and he wants to go home, and he doesn't understand why he can't go home to mum, and so it's hard to try and explain and for him to understand

that he needs some help, and mum isn't the one who can give the help right now, or ever, in this particular case. We need to find somebody who can help him, so that he can be safe and secure and be able to learn because he can't function in school. Both parents are involved, but they're both substance users and have some history and ... there's a general neglect of basic needs. This child ... wants to go home desperately. I used to tell him all the time and try and explain to him that he can't.'

N22 stated that she handled discrepancies in opinions like this: "It's through conversations and through information and contact that one can try to reach an agreement or not reach an agreement [with the child or young person]". N23 said that, in instances of disagreements, she explained to the child why she disagreed and highlighted "the reasons, the explanation why I believe what I believe". She conceded:

'It's often not heard. It's no secret that the children we work with, they often do not master demands so well and often become frustrated. So when that happens, when they meet resistance, they handle that poorly. And then they're not very receptive to my arguments, but I have faith in repeating things, because I understand that it's difficult to get a grasp on what they don't agree with, and they may not have full ... the prerequisite to understand, either. But repetitions are very important.'

Several participants' quotes evidenced that it takes engaged conversations, persistence and time on the workers' part to provide information and explanations about the agency's viewpoints and decisions. This is how C23 explained that she would not support children returning home to parents who were abusive, emotionally unavailable or had abandoned them:

'I know the children want to return [home]. I expect that. On the other hand, that's not something I'm going to recommend if I think it's going to hurt the child. So I would take the time to explain to the child, and I would talk with the foster parent to see whether she could reason with the child. I would talk to the child's attorney to see if they could reason with the child, and if we couldn't get any place, we couldn't get any place.'

Several study participants mentioned situations when they needed to explain to children why they needed to stay in their home despite their wish to leave. C26 mentioned how she does so:

> 'A lot of times we'll have to have family meetings and explain to the child why CPS [Child Protective Services] is not going to step in and remove that child even though they say they don't want to return to the parents' home because they're not getting along or whatever. That's not necessarily a CPS matter because there's not substantial risk in the home, or substantial abuse.'

The participants who provided information to children often, but not always, consulted them about their opinion or facilitated their participation by acting as children's spokespersons in meetings or reassuring them that their voice would be heard. This was primarily the case with participants in Norway. N2's quote illuminates how providing information about the case process can happen at the same time as asking children about their opinions and wishes. This is how N2 provides information to children and parents about the child protection agency's role and case process when she investigates a referral:

> 'And so we tend to ask whether they've been told about us, and then there's a part of them who says no, they haven't heard of us. But then we tell them who we are, in a straightforward way, that we are working with the parents, the children, to help them, yes ... But generally, we work a lot with the initial meetings. And prior to that we have to go to the home and talk with the children. We shall meet the family at home. And then ... we tell them that we'll have a kind of big meeting with many different people. And we tell them ... the teacher will be coming and things like that, so they know something about it. And then I always ask, "Is there anything I should bring up that you would like to be said, at the meeting? Is there anything that I should convey for you?".'

N11 clarified how she works with young people who are required to go into a residential home that focuses on substance use treatment but refuse to go. Her quote indicated how she allows young people to develop and express their viewpoints by engaging them in conversations:

'Talk, talk and talk with them. They say something about why they believe they don't need it, if you think [it's] a 24 [an intervention without the child's consent] and they think that they don't need it, so I spend a lot of time explaining why I as child welfare service [professional] believe that it may be good for them. How I work with young people, I expect that they'll say something back and they'll also be able to justify what they say. So we spend a lot of time on exchanging views about it and sometimes we don't agree, and then I spend some time on saying that the county board decides that. We disagree, then we let someone else decide. They're usually fine with it. Sometimes conflicts resolve themselves and they get simplified. We must be able to discuss it. They must also give their reasons why they don't need it.'

The following quotes illustrate how study participants reported providing emotional information to children by recognizing children's viewpoints and empathizing with their feelings when explaining the rationale behind decisions. C9 explained:

'So what I will do is make as clear as possible to the child why it's going contrary to the way they'd like it to go. I will recognize their disagreement; I will recognize their anger; I will recognize their pain, and I will do my best to relay that to the child. But I will also make it very clear that this is the only direction it's going to go right now.'

N24 mentioned how she signals recognition of children's feelings and wishes when disagreeing with youths who she must place in emergency placements:

'Often, we disagree very much, especially at the beginning, when we make an emergency placement. Because we often place ... they're often intoxicated, they often come, or sometimes, up from the police. And they don't want any help, they don't want to have any interference in their lives – they have it absolutely wonderful the way they have it! So then we use quite a lot of time to say that I understand that you're thinking that this is not okay, and I realize that you feel this way and that, but we're going to have to do this anyway.'

N5 described how she provided information about the child welfare agency's decision to a 14-year-old girl who wanted to stay with her mother but was removed from home by the child welfare agency: "Then I say that I hear what you're saying, and I understand it. I said that as recently as yesterday." N5 provided emotional information to the girl by validating her feelings about the situation. She elaborated:

> 'And I said to her that I know that she [wants to continue staying with her mum], and I understand that. You've lived there until now, and you love your mother. We know that. We believe that, [but] the child welfare service believes that it is harmful to you anyway … and then she is so big [old] that I'm honest and say why.'

In these examples, participants undertook what sociologist Ervin Goffman (1959) called 'impression management'. This is a way to control the impression individuals make on others. Goffman wrote that:

> it will be in [one party's] interest to control the conduct of others, especially their responsive treatment of him. This control is achieved largely by influencing the definition of the situation which the others come to formulate, and he can influence this definition by expressing himself in such a way as to give them the kind of impression that will lead them to act voluntarily in accordance with his own plan. (Goffman, 1959, p 4)

The participants who mentioned providing emotional information tried to signal to children that they cared about children's opinion and respected them. Impression management allowed the participants to support children in expressing their opinions and wishes. The impression management they undertook by empathizing with children's feelings and wishes (while at the same time deciding against them) could be interpreted as workers' way of coping with the daunting dilemma of expressing respect in a situation in which they cannot act on children's wishes because of the imperative to keep them safe.

This is important because a positive rapport between children and caseworkers has been identified as a ladder to participation in prior literature. Conversely, a lack of a respectful relationship between children and child protection professionals has been found to impede participation (Thomas and O'Kane, 1999a; Bell, 2002; Smith et al, 2003; Healy and Darlington, 2009; Pölkki et al, 2012; Vis et al, 2012;

Cossar et al, 2014; Paulsen, 2015, 2016; Burford and Gallagher, 2015; Arbeiter and Toros, 2017; Križ and Roundtree-Swain, 2017).

Facilitating participation

The quotations about workers who facilitated participation mostly evidenced Shier's first four participation levels (Shier, 2001): workers consulted with children and involved them in decision-making. Decisions based on collaboration between workers and children, or decisions initiated by children (Shier's final level five) were barely mentioned. Only one worker, C40, described a situation in which an older teen initiated and led a decision. This was a teenage girl who insisted on moving out of her mother's home and out of town for college, when C40 thought it would be best for her to attend college in town and build a relationship with her mother. Children were often presented with "choices" that were narrowly defined and within the boundaries of what workers considered to be within the parameter of children's best interests (especially their safety). Children often had a voice, were supported in making their voice heard and received information, and they even had some control over the process. During the investigative phase of a case, they had little power to make the decision about whether to stay with their family.

The participants in both countries mentioned ways in which they ensured that children could develop and express their wishes and views through a spokesperson in meetings with the child protection worker or in group meetings with parents and professionals. The following quotes evidence the ways in which workers said they consulted children about their opinions and wishes: C9, an investigator, simply said, "I will ask the child what they'd like to see different". C8, a manager, told us about interviews in her unit: "We ask children ... what they'd like to see happen; one of my workers' favourite questions is to say, 'If you had three wishes, what would they be?' at the end of an interview". Other workers discussed how children were consulted about placement choices when they were removed. C3 stated: "I may ask them: 'Is there a place you want to live if it's possible?' 'Are there relatives that you have?' 'What would you like to see happen if this can't happen? What's the next best thing?' So I think early on they're involved." C16 described what she said to a child when she interviewed them: "'OK, we know you can no longer live with mum. Give me the name of your favourite auntie or favourite cousin who you might want to live with'." C37 noted:

'Especially if we're talking about an alternative to where they're going to live, then it's important to involve them, if appropriate. If it's a very young child, then it's probably not appropriate. If you've got a couple of relatives, and as the worker you'd place them with either of them and they both want the child, then it might be a good idea to talk to the child about what would make them more comfortable, and maybe there could be shared co-parenting with the relative.'

The extent to which children were consulted and the choices they were offered were circumscribed by the severity of a case: if workers assessed children's safety to be at risk, then their judgement overrode children's wishes. This occurred in situations where a child would have liked to remain in an abusive or neglectful home. This did not mean that children were prevented from making other choices. N10 explained it like this:

'If our assessment is that placing the child [out of home] is the only thing we can do, if we have an emergency situation, if it is a placement, then I would probably not have asked about it. Then I would better let the child influence other things: what kind of place would you like to stay in if you were able to choose? Should it be someone who has pets? Should it be someone who lives in the city? A child once had a wish ... she very much wanted a cow "If they have a cow, I'm in!".'

C2 recalled how she gave a seven-year-old girl on her caseload the opportunity to develop an opinion and express her wish in a case where three siblings were removed because of neglect. She mentioned how doing so helped her better engage with the girl:

'And I explained to [the children] what was going to happen. "Well, you know what? Your mum's gotta go now and she asked me to help find you guys a place", and ... "What would you like to have in a new house?". And I remember the kid telling me – she was seven years old – and she goes, "I want my own bed". Because up to that point they all slept in one bed, including the baby ... And I go, "Really? What would you like on your bed?". And so she told me. And when we got to the house ... and we went into the bedroom, not only did each girl have their own bed, but they also had their own bathroom inside the bedroom … She looked at me and she goes, "Thank you! Thank you! That's all I want" … I knew for a fact she was going to get her own bed because that's the law … But for her, that was a biggie. And the fact that she was able to express it, to be able to say that's what she wanted, and that's what she got, I think helped her. Because every time I would come, I asked her things … and little by little she was able to come out of her shell.'

The participants stated that they told children about their rights to express their views, either individually or through a spokesperson, such as a lawyer in court or county board hearings. N2 told us how she consulted with children about their opinions prior to meetings so she could act as a spokesperson in the meetings on their behalf:

'And then I always ask, "Is there anything I should bring up that that you would like to be said, at the meeting? Is there anything that I should convey for you?". And then … they can say that they would like to have less conflict at home. Some wish for more friends. Some want the bullying to end. These kinds of things.'

N7 said that when discussing cases of disagreement, she says: "Here you disagree, and you should have your lawyer, and you should promote your view of the matter". C12 explained that rather than disagreeing with children outright, she prefers to ask them questions because disagreement usually stops children from listening: "Once you say I don't agree with you, you have the makings of an argument and nobody hears anything". She continued to explain her approach:

'So I would engage them in a conversation to really give them the opportunity to participate in their self-determination. And then if I really thought it was a safety issue, again, depending on the child's age and development, I would say, "I'm sorry, I can't really support that. But you have an attorney, and I will get you an appointment with your attorney, and I will take you to his office if you want me to, or get your foster parent to take you to his office, and I'll let him know that you and I disagree about this, and you can tell him, because he's your voice in the courtroom".'

N16 reflected on the usefulness of children working with a lawyer. She said she valued the importance of another set of eyes on her decision as a form of checks and balances on her work. She found that involving a lawyer had helped her arrive at solutions for the child in the past:

> 'I respect that the child has an opinion, but I will come with my decision anyway, an assessment of what I believe will be the best. And then I think that someone must run some quality assurance on me. A team manager, a county board bureaucracy, someone else. I've often asked young people to consult a lawyer, and I found that a lawyer is supposed to listen to what the child, their client, says and thinks, but they also use common sense, and we can often arrive at solutions.'

The study participants discussed how they asked children about choices of services. When asked about how she involved a child, N7 replied: "They're asked and talked with in advance about how they see the situation, what they're thinking and what types of support they can imagine". C33 told us that during an investigation she usually asks children about which extracurricular activities they would like to pursue: "If they don't have anything that they like or do and we're connecting them with services, we'll ask them, 'What types of things do you like, like sports or art? Is counselling something you would like, to talk to somebody?' And most of the time they say yes."

A few of the study participants mentioned that they facilitated participation by asking children's opinions on how and how much they'd like to be involved. They allowed children some control over process in this way. N11 stated:

> 'From the first call when they're given the report, and they know why this is a child welfare case, they can say something about it and whether they recognize themselves in the report. They can also help control the investigation; how we should arrange it; they'll have the opportunity to decide whether they'll meet here [in the office], whether they want us to meet at home or at school or elsewhere.'

This way of creating participation included workers respecting children's wishes *not* to talk to the worker or in a meeting or to participate in a decision. C24, an investigator, thought that it was important "to respect [children] if they don't want to talk, and to let them know that it's okay, that if there is a danger in the family, where they're going to be hurt, that I may have to make a decision. And I explain that decision". Even if the child chooses not to participate, C24 still thought that giving information to the child was important.

N25 described how she gauged a boy's wishes about letting the child protection agency make the decision about the frequency of visits with his parents:

> 'When I had the boy that I was talking about, he was heard, and we took the decision that he should be placed. I remember that I once talked with him then, so I used a few of these marbles, it was a method I had learned, as if throwing them into a glass. I used only three marbles then and I said, "If you strongly agree that it's awesome what I'm saying, then you throw three marbles into the glass. If you somewhat agree, then throw two marbles, and if you disagree, then you throw one marble." And then I asked him exactly that question that applied to the visitation because he thought it was hard to say how often he wanted to meet with the parents; it seems that's often the case. Then I said to him, "If I say to you that the child welfare agency will decide how much interaction you're going to have with dad," for example, so I sat there and explained how this was then, "how many marbles would you throw up then?". Then he took three marbles and threw them up in one swoop, and that said everything; it was what he wanted, he wanted us to decide. Some things are too difficult for them. So I also used that some other times with children, and I see that sometimes what they want is that there is someone else who decides.'

These quotes show that many of the study participants encouraged consultative participation: they listened to children and supported them in expressing their opinions and wishes. They also promoted collaborative participation: they took children's views into account and involved them in decision-making processes. The decisions in which children were collaborators were decisions about foster placements, extracurricular activities and services, and how and to what degree children wanted to be involved. They never involved the decision about whether to remove the child from home. This was clearly a decision in which children had no power. This illustrates again that the stage in a case is crucial to the degree and matter in which a child protection worker involves a child. In an investigation, children have no autonomy to decide (about the removal), nor do they have much of a voice other than to provide information. They do receive information about what is happening and what their rights are, and there is evidence that they are supported in expressing their wishes and views. They may have a choice in whether to participate and thus have some control over the process. Children seem to gain in autonomy, choice of participating *and* voice once the decision about removal has been made.

Gathering information

All the participants stated that they or their agency involved children from the very beginning of a case, right after a referral about alleged abuse or neglect reached the child protection agency. The participants in both countries mentioned that they sought information from children to gather evidence, build rapport, get to know children and engage them. They sought to understand the feelings or thoughts behind the child's perspective and views. One worker (C30) mentioned gathering information for the purpose of assessing the child's development. Participants mentioned that they gathered evidence by asking questions and by observing children's daily interactions and body language in the home, at school or in individual meetings at the child protection agency.

The percentage of participants who mentioned gathering information was higher in California than in Norway. This was likely the case because many of the participants there worked in emergency response units. Gathering information to them meant 'interviewing' children to assess the risk to the child's safety. These participants were focused on gathering evidence in a short period of time to investigate what had happened that could pose a risk to the child, so they could determine whether they had to remove the child from the home. It is noteworthy that the investigating workers interviewed in Norway and several investigating workers in California explicitly stated that, when gathering evidence, they took a holistic, strengths-based approach. This is a type of social work approach that looks at a family's strengths and resilience factors, not only their deficiencies (Child Welfare Information Gateway, 2008). They reported gathering information about the child's social environment, their family network and the positive circumstances and events in a child's life to assess how to best support the child and the child's caregivers.

The following quotes exemplify the different purposes of information gathering. The study participants stated that they gathered information from and about children verbally and by observing children, especially when children were still pre-verbal. N17 explained that during an investigation, "when it comes to children who are so small that they're not verbal, from three years and down, we'll always observe. We'll do a home visit where we see the parents and the children together." N12 said that:

'I often "talk" through pen and paper, colours, watching and being together with children in their environment, looking at their room, getting descriptions of what they have around them in their rooms … drawing and explaining their family network a little, drawing the house, drawing who lives there, their pets.'

C39 said, "we always interview the kid or at least see a child; if you have a baby, of course they're not going to talk to you; but you have to look at their injuries and also take into consideration where their injuries are and that kind of thing". C40 stated that:

'If I get a child who's two, three years old, I involve them by doing my investigation … Some kids are not able to talk and so the involvement is a little bit hampered by their inability to communicate, but in terms of investigations, sometimes I have to look at their bodies and see bruises; I have to take them places … and have them assessed medically and all that.'

The following quotes show the information-gathering approach used by emergency response workers in California. When asked at what stages she involved children, C26 replied, "especially from the front end [of a case], we do it right away. From the minute we get the case, we interview the children and assess the situation." C1 stated: "I interview the child right away and try to get their sense of what's going on, and to see their worldview, and to see if they can share or are open to sharing information with me". C13 said: "I actively listen to the child and try to figure out what the main issues are". This is how C4 described how she involved children in an investigation by interviewing them:

'I usually start off by just trying to find out, get a general sense of what they're like: what grade they're in, what their routine is like at home, who's in their home. And then we start talking about rules … most of the time, I'm going out there because it's a physical discipline situation or some sort of neglect ... those are kind of the two main ones. And then we get into discipline and how is it ... who's the disciplinarian, who gets disciplined; do they get disciplined the same? And the questions that I ask are open-ended, so they're not leading. I let them fill it in. And with the fighting, for example, when I'm trying to assess DV [domestic violence], I usually ask, "Does anybody argue in the house? Who, you know, who, and how do they argue? Do they argue with their hands, or with their mouth?".'

C16, an emergency response worker in California, emphasized that children's participation at the front end of a case was limited to information gathering:

'At the front end, you are just doing the interviewing of the child. The child does not participate in very much else unless you're saying, "Okay, we know you can no longer live with mum. Give me the name of your favourite auntie or your favourite cousin who you might want to live with". Or, "Tell me why it's better for you to be with dad than mum." But other than that, we just do investigations.'

C5, another emergency response worker, said that:

'Our work goes very quickly; we may only see the children once. If it's a situation where we determine there's no risk or very little risk, or the only thing that remains to be done is to talk to the parents about what they might be changing or what services they might avail themselves of, then we won't need to see the kids again. Times when we do need to see the kids possibly again is if we're going to remove [them], and we don't remove them right away.'

The time-sensitive, limited nature of children's participation during this very early investigation stage of a case, especially in California, is made clear in the following quote by C28. The participants described one of her investigations:

'A nine-year-old in school [states] that he was hit on his legs with a belt for ongoing misbehaviours in the classroom setting. We would talk to the child, get the child to feel comfortable to show us the marks or bruising. We ascertain whether or not he's hit with the leather part of the belt or with the belt buckle, whether or not the skin is broken, whether or not there's marks targeted on the legs or on the behind, or whether it's indiscriminate where the child was also hit close enough to the eye. We would ask the frequency of it, when was the last time it occurred, why do you think it happened, or what happened? Is it every Tuesday and Thursday night, he or she gets a beating for no reason at all? The level of fear that the child is experiencing, how it impacts the child also in terms of whether or not he's able to sleep or eat or et cetera. Whether or not it impacts how the child behaves in school. But just to determine the level of fear on behalf of the child, and if it's a high degree of fear, it's very realistic that perhaps the child should not be returning home that particular evening. And then of course we look at history; whether or not there's been any prior abuse reports. What safety factors can we put in place if the child goes home?'

This is how C9 explained how she involved children in an investigation:

'One of the things I have to determine is if the allegations [made in a report to the child protection agency] were true or not; to what extent they may or may not be true. For example, in physical abuse cases I will involve a child to determine whether there was a deliberate act by the parent to cause pain and suffering to the children ... I'll ask the child what they'd like to see different. I will solicit from them what their perception is about their family, which may or may not be working, and how they think that might be changed. I will solicit from them what their needs are.'

The purpose of speaking with the child in an investigation is assessment of risk: "in investigations, we're all about child safety, but doing the investigation with the ... minor is only part of it". C29 noted that observing the child's behaviour is part of the structured decision-making she's using in an investigation: "It's on our structured decision-making, what the child's behaviour is, it's on there". Structured decision-making (SDM) is a decision-making tool based on research evidence used by workers in California. This tool guides workers in assessing the risk to the child and determining the interventions (D'Andrade et al, 2008; Berrick Duerr et al, 2015a).

Other purposes of gathering information included getting to know and engaging the child, assessing the child's development, and understanding the feelings and reflections behind the child's opinions and wishes. Two Norwegian study participants mentioned employing 'The River of Life' tool (mentioned in Chapter 1), which guides workers through asking children to describe their life; this tool allows workers to get to know and build rapport with the child and their perspective on their life and family. N21 stated that:

> 'we've recently used a method called The River of Life to get an idea of the experiences they remember and what pleasures they have in life, things that have been difficult ... from birth; it's things they remember, things they did together [with their family], which is a very safe and straightforward way in which to connect with kids; they forget a little that we're strangers.'

N28 explained: "One lays these rivers side by side; mum has hers and the child has hers; it takes time ... And it has been shown that both in the investigation it's quite useful but also along the way; to get to know the child."

The following quotes show how the participants gathered information to understand a child's reasoning and feelings about a situation. C8 discussed one of her cases, where she "had to get to the problem behind the problem" to figure out why a little boy expressed certain wishes. Through conversations with him she found out he felt responsible for his parents' divorce. N3 mentioned the case of an eight-year-old boy who had been removed from home and did not want to visit his mother: "So you'll have to try to find out why the child doesn't want that. What's the reason for it? Is it because he's afraid to go away from mum's [after the visit]?" Several workers mentioned that children may not express certain opinions and wishes because they feel loyal towards their parents and fear they may be harming their parents if they disclosed information. Similar dynamics related to loyalty conflicts were found by a Finnish study of foster children by Pölkki et al (2012). N15's quote illustrates how N15 gathers information about children's feelings about their situation. N15 employs a strengths-based approach in doing so. It shows that asking children about their wishes and opinions can be a stepping stone towards their participation in decision-making:

> '[When a child's opinion differs from mine], I try to think about what it is that leads to those statements. I cannot say

that a child is lying either, but [clearly] I think through what needs the child fulfils when she says what she does ... Is it to protect [her parents]? Children are largely very loyal. And that's part of what being a kid is, too. But, it's not always the most important thing for me that a child confirms how bad she has it. It may be my job to consider ... but ... a conversation might as well be about that which is good in your life and what we can do even better. Is there anything that can help you get to master it even more? Or ... you're saying that my mum is so good at that; how can we get so that we're going to get even more of that? Because we cannot interrogate children to bring up all the misery, in a way. It comes when it comes, what they want to say ... Many of the conversations are not like, "oh god, I have it so bad", but what is good in life and what we can do even better?'

The purpose of N15's conversation with the child was not only to gather information to assess whether the child was safe. N15 asked the child to reflect on their situation and develop an opinion about what they would like to see changed.

C32 described how she used to gather information about foster children's views on their situation when she was an ongoing worker:

'And I would certainly get input from them on what they thought their lives were like and who their friends were, and how they felt about their foster parents or the people they were living with, and their schools ... because you don't see them all that often, and you want to know from them how are things going and what's going on with you.'

Conclusion

The study participants reported involving children in a variety of ways, for different purposes. They gathered information from children, gave information to children, and facilitated children's participation. The most frequently mentioned approach to involving children, mentioned by 60 per cent of the study participants, was providing information to children. Study participants reported giving different kinds of information to children. They provided emotional information by signalling to children that they recognized their feelings and wishes, often in situations when they decided against children's wishes. They offered logistical information by telling children about the case process and the worker's and agency's role and responsibilities. Some of the participants reported providing empowering information when they assured children that their opinions and wishes would be heard in the child protection process and when they acted as the child's spokesperson in meetings. This corresponds with one of Thomas's (2002) bricks in the climbing wall – supporting children in voicing their wishes and opinions. Norwegian workers were more likely to report giving empowering information to children. This could be because the principle for the child to be heard is explicitly stated in Norwegian law. It could be because the Californian sample was skewed towards investigators in an emergency response unit.

Overall, a little less than 50 per cent of the participants mentioned how they facilitated children's genuine participation. Children's degree of genuine participation in decision-making remained at the lower levels. By Lansdown's (2010) typology, most of children's participation reported by the study participants was consultative (and not collaborative or child-initiated) participation. The decisions that study participants consulted children about were restricted to specific situations and decisions. They reported consulting children about where they wanted to meet, about choices related to visits and foster home arrangements, but not about removals from home. In situations in which workers had to assess expeditiously whether a child was at imminent risk of harm, the protection principle upended the principle of participation. This evidences the tension between the paternalistic imperative of child protection systems and children's participatory rights – one of the many competing principles that child protection workers need to bridge in their daily practice, as Berrick Duerr's work on the practice of Californian child protection workers has shown (Berrick Duerr, 2018).

Forty per cent of the overall sample of study participants reported gathering information, often in the form of evidence during an investigation into a referral of child maltreatment. The participants gathered information about a child's views and feelings about their situation, got to know and engaged with the child, and evaluated the child's level of development. Interestingly, both gathering information from children and providing information to children was linked to consultative participation in the participants' responses. Information (gathering and giving), as an element of communication and building rapport, emerged as a central stepping stone towards participation. This approach resonates with the findings of prior research on children's experiences with participation. This research showed that children perceive receiving information as an important pathway to participation, and the lack thereof as a daunting hurdle (Thomas and O'Kane, 1999a; Skivenes and Strandbu, 2006; Pölkki et al, 2012; Eidhammer, 2014; van Bijleveld et al, 2014; Burford and Gallagher, 2015; Balsells et al, 2017; Križ and Roundtree-Swain, 2017).

The workers interviewed in California were more likely to report gathering evidence during an investigation of child maltreatment than workers in Norway. In an analysis of the same study participants (but using responses to more of the interview questions), Archard and Skivenes (2009b) also showed that workers' listening approach was instrumentalist as it served the purpose of assessing the risk to the child or needs of the child. This finding could be explained by the fact that many of the study participants in California were working in emergency response units, whereas the workers interviewed in Norway were more evenly divided between investigative and ongoing workers. It could reflect the protective orientation and adversarial, legalistic approach of the US child protection system (Berrick Duerr, 2011).

6

Youth citizens

In the Introduction (Chapter 1), I discussed the link between children's participation and children's status as citizens. Citizens are persons who are able and are given the opportunity to participate in decisions that affect their lives and the lives of their communities. These participatory opportunities can be written into the law, through formal rights to participation. They can also be created in interactions between children and adults. Thus, child protection professionals are in a position where they can help engender children's fully-fledged citizenship status by promoting their participation in their interactions with them. Child protection caseworkers make very important decisions about children's lives, including removal from home into out-of-home care, the type of out-of-home care and other services a child, young person and family need to keep the child safe. In this chapter I show that study participants view and often treat youths as citizens by providing them with opportunities for consultative, if not collaborative or child-led, participation.

As Chapter 4 showed, many of the study participants stated that the extent to which they involved teenagers differed from younger children: teens were more likely to participate in decisions about removal, foster placements, parental visits, and reunification. The threshold between the children who obtained information but could not decide and those who were consulted and whose statements and opinions were taken seriously appeared to be the cusp of adolescence. The average age of the children who participants mentioned when they described situations in which the child's opinion significantly mattered was 12.6 years for Norway and 13 years for California. This chapter builds on this finding and focuses on the study participants' perceptions of and experiences with involving teenagers. In what ways did they involve teens differently from younger children? What did they perceive as the challenges when involving teens? How did they resolve these challenges? The analysis for this chapter shows that participants in both countries conceptualized teens as children who possess power – they described them as defiant, rebellious, and resisting interventions. The findings of this chapter also suggest that child protection caseworkers' negative perception of a teen as lying and manipulative, a type of perception primarily evident in the Californian data, might indirectly recognize teen power.

This chapter rests on study participants' responses to two interview questions: "At which stages in a case do you involve children?" and "How do you proceed when a child's opinion and wishes were different from your own views?". In their response to these questions, 63 per cent of the overall sample (or 43 out of 68 study participants) indicated that a child's age affected how they involved children during an investigation, when they removed the child from home, and when they implemented services. A little over half (54 per cent or 15 out of 28) Norwegian study participants (N) and 70 per cent (or 28 out of 40) study participants in California (C) indicated that the way in which they involved children depended on their age. The study participants empowered pre-teens and teens (12 years and older) more so than younger children by involving them differently. Many participants said that they would meet or talk with teens earlier in the stage of a case and on their own, were more honest about the issues in a case, asked teens different questions, and gave them more substantive choices and influence over decisions. In the following, I shall describe how the study participants reported promoting participation when working with teens.

Earlier involvement and more substantial choices

Four of the study participants in Norway mentioned that older children were involved earlier on in the case process: they received their own letter about the report to the child protection agency; they were contacted before the parents; and they were present in the first meeting with the worker and parent(s). N4 stated that when young people were concerned, they were involved in an investigation very early on: "They're involved starting in the first hour of the case. They get a copy of the letter saying that an investigation was initiated. It's the exception if they're not present at the first conversation." N23 put it like this: "So, given that I work with youth now and have done for so many years, I involve them right away. They are the protagonists, and it's the child we should be working for ... I often contact the youth before I make contact with the parents." N16, who mostly works with youth as well, said that during an investigation: "I'll always contact the youth and ... I say something about who I am, why I've contacted them, and I invite them to the conversation ... the vast majority want to come here to the office; there are very few who want us to come to their home." N7 was asked at which stage of the case process she would involve the child. She responded:

> 'Relatively early. For younger children, I would wait. When we're notified about a 15-year-old and we convene the first meeting, then the 15-year-old will be there for the first meeting as a rule. For a five-year-old, that's not as normal. Then that's the point to go over concerns about the parents first, together, and then talk to parents about ways to talk with the child.'

When asked why she would wait to involve a five-year-old (but not a 15-year-old), N7 explained:

> 'For the five-year-old it can revolve around the five-year-old's behaviour; it can also revolve around parental care capabilities. But [we must be able] to take the parents' reactions and have an adult chat without the child hearing it. For the 15-year-old, it's almost invariably linked to what the 15-year-old engages in or does or did. And then the point is not to go behind the back of the 15-year-old. I feel less like going behind the [older] child's back than when I talk with a five-year-old. Because the parent has a little more responsibility to safeguard both the five-year-old's everyday life, and could also give us some input through the way [they] talk to the five-year-old.'

This quote suggests that older children may be consulted more based on the expectation that they must take responsibility for their own behaviour, a sentiment echoed by other study participants.

Several participants in both countries mentioned that they involved children differently during an investigation depending on their age: they observed younger children and talked with older children. C29 told us that she observes the behaviour of younger children (the children in her examples were an infant and a two-year-old) to identify problems, following the SDM tool that workers in California employ to gauge risk. C19 mentioned that children's maturity played a role in how she involved them:

> 'it depends on their developmental maturity, because some, at age five, they don't want to talk to us, they [say,], "I don't

know, I don't know", and all they do is cry or they get mad, and then it's really hard. But some kids I've seen at age five and they can say, "I don't want this, but I want this".'

C20 noted that she would talk with children older than three:

'maybe not two or three – it would be difficult to get their involvement, but I can ... I mean, not so much them giving me an opinion, but really considering what's best for this child ... But I think in terms of active involvement, I would say if cognitively they're ready to give me their opinion, their ideas, talk to me or give me some direction, I will take it. Because they're the victim.'

C4 explained that she involved children in an investigation "right away; because we have to interview them. So, if they're listed in the referral, we're mandated to see them and assess them for an interview. So obviously, if you need to [assess] a six-month-old, you eyeball them, and you look at them and see that they're okay, but you're not going to interview them." N17, too, mentioned that she observed, rather than talked with, very young children in an investigation: "When it comes to children who're so small that they're not verbal, from three years and down, we'll always observe ... We'll do a home visit where we see the parents and children together." N12 stated that, "when it's very small children, it's more like seeing them in interaction". Several workers mentioned that they observe older children in their daily interactions with family as well, not only speak with them. C8 explained her role in an investigation and ended her description with:

'So that is the level of involvement I would get children involved in initially, and then depending on what the issue was I would touch base back with them maybe [but] not necessarily ... it just depends on how old the child is, too. If you have a teenager, it's going to look a whole lot different than if you have a little kid.'

Children 12 years and older were given more substantial choices by child protection workers, whereas choices for younger children were limited and defined by the workers. C30 mentioned modifying her questions about choices and parental behaviour depending on the age of the child in the context of talking about three- or four-year-old children: "If they don't know, I won't ask them difficult questions like 'Want to be home with your parents?' or 'What are your parents doing?' If there's something they want to tell me, they'll voice it." C32 said this about how she involves children:

'In general, I would try to get some involvement from them appropriate to their developmental stage. So, they're not making big decisions when they're four or five, but they might make a decision about what we're going to do when I come to visit them, or what colour dress they're going to wear when they go visit mum, something. And I would certainly get input from them on what they thought their lives were like and who their friends were and how they felt about their foster parents or the people they were living with and their schools when they had schools. Because you don't see them all that often, and you want to know from them, how are things going and what's going on with you.'

C37 insisted that children were involved starting from the very beginning of a case, especially in removal situations, and then she quickly qualified her statement: "and especially if we're talking about an alternative to where they're going to live, then it's important to involve them, if appropriate. If it's a very young child, then it's probably not appropriate." C39 replied that when she disagreed with a child, "depending on the kid's age, I always try to talk to the child about what's going on with them, what we're planning and why we can't do some things; at least I try to explain".

Teenagers were given the opportunity to develop choices and then substantially influence which options they could choose. According to C7, "[when we work with teenagers], we ask them, 'OK, is this bad enough? Do you want to go home, or do you want to go to a foster home? Let's talk about what a foster home would be like'." C39 replied, "for kids who're older, we're supposed to invite them to the TDM". C35 said that she involved children:

'from the very beginning ... in the initial TDM. If possible, again depending on the age, but especially, most TDMs, they are for placement issues [that is related to placing a child in care], and we'd like the child to be aware of what the placement choices are and why and what we expect out of them. So, we try and do it from the beginning here.'

C5 said that older children were sometimes (but not always) invited: "They're often not invited, but sometimes, if they're teenagers, it might make sense once in a while for them to be able to say what they want to say at one of those meetings". She later specified that "it would be a specialized case where the children would be invited" to a meeting, and that the children need to be mature enough "to deal with what was going on, what was being said" in the meeting to be invited. This indicates that not all workers would invite teens to meetings about their case. When asked how older children would be involved in a TDM, C5 explained:

'They would just be one of the people that sits around ... we have a big conference table, and everybody puts up their name card and who they are or how they're associated, how they came to the table, why, so it would be their first name and whatever, and ... they would be asked to join in. There's a certain format to the meetings. First, they ... ask the parents to tell, talk about their children ... what they like to do and that kind of thing, and then they get to the issues as much as possible in terms of why we're there, what brought us to the table, what the referral involves, and then we talk about what we can do to address those issues. So, these are all sheets of paper, and there's a facilitator up at the front of the room, and it's done in an orderly fashion.'

Two of the Norwegian workers mentioned that 12-year-olds and 15-year-olds had the right to participation by law; in fact, 15-year-olds were considered a party under the law. C19 said that she involved children at the age of "ten, because they can go to court". Then she added, "But it doesn't mean we don't talk to kids if they're four or five, when the child can articulate what he or she wants".

Several participants stated that they communicated differently with older children. C22 emphasized honesty when she described how she would talk with young people about differences in opinions:

C22: 'Once again, with a teenager, I tell them straight out and straightforward, this is how it is. You can decide to walk away, do this, to not participate, whatever, this is your life. So, I just tell them that you do have the control in this situation, I'm not going to walk after you ... So, it's important that you get on board with whatever, or your life is

116

	still going to be the same. I just kind of point out the consequences and what's going on. Now, with little children, I mean …'
Interviewer:	'What are little children?'
C22:	'Little children, under ten. Children under ten that are school age. If you can still pick them up, you can pretty much control them. You just have to talk to them about "I know you don't agree, you're sad, this hurts you, blah, blah, blah, but we have to make this decision for you and you're not going to like it, but I promise it'll get better". You just try to smooth it over.'

This quote indicates that the study participant thinks of children older than ten years as less controllable or more powerful. One of the Californian participants, C21, emphasized that older children should be involved:

> 'from the very first time you meet them; otherwise it's just pointless. And I think you should be honest … from the very beginning. If they say to you, "Are you going to take me away?" – that's when you should start being truthful to them. So, right from the beginning. It's more age for me than situation; I wouldn't necessarily have that conversation … I would have a simpler version of it with a three-year-old or a four-year-old, but not so much ask them, "What do you want?".'

C24 underlined that "I think that being very clear from the beginning, depending on the age, gives the children an opportunity to maybe reconsider. And they become more engaging." C27 described the straightforward language she used with children if there were differences in opinion:

> 'I usually let them know what the next action is that I'm going to take and, depending on the child's maturity and age, I will say that may lead to these other subsequent actions … So, I usually let them know … I'm worried about you getting hit by your mother again when she's drunk, and I'm just not comfortable with you staying there with her right now. So right now, maybe you should go stay with your grandma.'

N7 and N5 stated that they were more honest with older children. N5 mentioned the case of a 14-year-old who wanted to stay in her mother's home but was moved to a foster home. N5 told the teen that she knew that she loved her mother, but she'd have to be moved anyway because it would be harmful for her to stay with her.

Workers' perceptions of teens

The study participants often mentioned challenges when working with teenagers. Their descriptions of these challenges partly differed across countries. Several Norwegian and Californian participants described teens as people who have the power to resist the child protection agency's interventions to the point of rendering them ineffective. Some of the participants in California described some of the teens they worked with as manipulative, lying and ego-driven. (Two of these workers did not mention teenagers or older children in specific cases.) The perceptions that the study participants drew on sometimes affected their involvement strategies: when workers thought of teenagers as children who are powerful enough to resist an intervention, they would follow the child's lead in decision-making. The understanding of teens as "defiant" could lead to collaborative or child-led participation, but there is evidence from two Californian study participants that it did not. The study participants who perceived teens as manipulative and lying did not appear to take teens' opinions seriously.

Several study participants mentioned that working with teenagers had its challenges. N27 described a divergence of opinion with young people as "painful" and "difficult" in the context of mentioning the child's age. When N22 was asked which dilemmas arose when she disagreed with the views expressed by a child, she responded like this:

> 'A dilemma in relation to youth, at least when young people are 15 years old, they're also their own parties in the case. It's clear that parents and young people can have very different experiences and very different needs, and it happens of course that we can come in between them many times, that it may be difficult to determine in a way what is the best for the young person and for family.'

When asked how she would proceed when her opinion differed from that of the child, C32 replied:

'It depends. Sometimes I'm certainly prone to doing this, "Okay, that's your opinion, but I'm the boss, and so it kind of depends on what you're clashing about." Usually I would try to explain, and if I disagreed, I would try to explain why I disagreed and why we were doing it my way, or why we needed to do it my way, or why what they wanted to do wasn't going to work for them or the system or their siblings or whatever it was that they wanted. That often doesn't work out very well, particularly with teenagers.'

A few of the study participants in both countries described teens as defiant or rebellious. C23 drew a distinction between younger children and teenagers when she described what children's participation meant to her. She depicted teenagers as children who have very strong opinions that are not necessarily in their best interests – something they do not always realize; therefore, they may resist the decisions made by the child protection agency. She explained, "Occasionally, we have kids that are older who are able to participate. Many times, their decision-making overlooks certain risk factors that would put them in jeopardy, and you can't convince them of it because ... I'm talking about the defiant teens."

The study participants who perceived teens as defiant thought that the case outcome would be more positive with the rebellious teenagers' "buy-in". These participants reasoned that young people would be more likely to engage in services, such as mental health services or substance use disorder treatments, and less likely to run away (from home or foster care), act out or cause "resistance" to other interventions by the child protection agency if they had a say. N15 emphasized the challenges of removing older children from home if they did not want to leave: "To move a 15-year-old is especially difficult because they run back home. And we have many examples of that." N14 thought that older children should be heard in the placement process; otherwise the child protection agency's intervention might not have the desired effect: "If you think, for example, that a youth should be placed somewhere ... it depends very much on the child having an experience of being heard as far as possible, and could affect ... the desired effect". She recounted the case of a girl who was removed from home against her wish. The girl reacted with "extreme behaviour" and "too much resistance" (N14) and as a result was moved back home. N14 explicated further:

'there's too much of this kind of resistance unless you're able, or the kids are able, to first ... reach acceptance to land where they are, because that's important ... so they can relax there [in the foster home] and accept the help they can get there. That's often a very, very [big] precondition so that, for example, a foster home measure or any other type of measure can be successful or become optimal. But if the child resists — it happens — resists and resists and fails to receive [help], then it becomes futile. We've seen that several times.'

C21, in a similar vein, explained why she thought it was important to let children participate (she did not specifically mention teens):

'I think they should have a say in what they want to do. Kids are going to vote with their feet. We do this in TDMs all the time: we'll say to the kid, "We want you to go there", and they'll say, "I'm not going there!". Now, why would we put them there if they're going to run? It's just going to create more problems. I think you have to find a place where they're willing to stay. So, in that way I definitely think they should participate.'

C15's response illustrated how workers perceive teenagers differently from younger children. We asked C15 how she would proceed when her opinion differed from the child's. This is what she said:

'I think it just really depends on the case, it depends on the age of the child, and it depends on the situation. I mean, many times I disagree with teens, because I think teens are coming from that teen mind, and nobody's going to make them happy, whether it's their parents, or whether it's that they think that the grass is greener on the other side ... so, all I can do is try to continue to help the kid ... keep an open mind. I've got a particular case now, they're pre-teens, and I can't verify whether their legal guardian, their grandma, actually really physically abused them. Yes, inappropriate physical discipline, absolutely. Yet, they are so adamant about not wanting any contact with her, and not wanting to talk to her, that I just keep trying to stress the fact that they're a family, and ultimately, when this all is said and done, and we go away, and they grow up, she's still going to be their grandma. And she loves them to death. And this is part of the process. And, you know ... I talk to them about communication, meaning that, didn't matter whether it was their parents, they would probably still feel the same way, that nobody understands them, they can't communicate, I mean it's all the classic things, but I just keep trying to bring it back to the fact that it's their family, and you just keep trying to work it that way while you implement services to kind of break down those barriers and those walls for a squeak of a chance to have them see things a little differently.'

This quote shows, unlike other quotes, that C15 thought that she could convince the child to change a preference. A similar approach was taken by C33. C33 used the adjective "rebellious" to describe teens and pre-teens who wanted to move away from home. She felt that she could convince teens of her viewpoint. This is how she reported working with rebellious teens and pre-teens:

'There are some kids who just want to ... like, they'll be clear that there's no abuse going on, but they just want to live with a friend ... or they're tired [of living with their parent(s)]. Kind of rebellious teens or tweens, young ones, 11 and 12, and just tell them that the rule is that your mum is your guardian, and you have to live at home until you are 18, and just to go over those ... I try to get them to see some viewpoints that they do like; some things that they like about their home environment; how awful it is on the other side, like the foster care system, and that they do have a good thing. So just to keep encouraging them, and telling them that this is the law, that they have to return back home, but in a soft manner.'

One worker, C40, mentioned that she tended to ask teenagers many questions about what their thought process is because "it forces them to think things through, and then sometimes when it's off, they sit there, and they get the picture". She continued:

'So through just being very inquisitive with kids: "What are you talking about?" "Why do you want that?" Children in their teenage years, they're learning to become adults, they're not there yet, that's the whole process, and so a lot of time they have erroneous thinking, and by me asking questions and being curious about what it is that they're trying to do, then it forces them to kind of reconsider everything they they've formulated. I'm very curious, especially with teens, I do it a lot.'

C40 conceived of teens as somewhat limited in their capacity to reason. C40 sometimes let older children develop an opinion through trial and error when they resisted an intervention. C40 discussed a case of a teen who had been in care and was reunited with her mother. The teen wanted to leave town to go to college, but C40 thought it would be better if she rebuilt her relationship with her mother and attended a local college. The teen ended up leaving anyway and, according to C40, "failed miserably". C40 said, "sometimes I let them, if it's teens, sometimes they have to learn because sometimes they can be really set [in their opinion]; so, I let them experience a little bit and see". This section showed that the labels 'defiant' and 'rebellious' to describe a teenager can lead to teens getting more empowered, but teens' resistance can be futile in changing their caseworker's opinion or decision.

Marit Skivenes and I analyzed the same study participants' responses to the interview question, "What is your understanding of participation in child protection?" We were surprised to find that quite a few workers in California (but not Norway) depicted teenagers as manipulative and lying in response to this question (Križ and Skivenes, 2015). I analyzed the interview responses of the same sample of study participants but looking at different interview questions for this book. This second analysis showed that quite a few study participants in California expressed less trust in teenagers than younger children and suggested that teens tended to lie to and manipulate their parents and their caseworkers to achieve what they wanted. Eleven of the Californian study participants (or 27.5 per cent of the participants who responded to the two interview questions I analyzed for this chapter), and only one Norwegian participant described teens who lied or manipulated their parents or caseworker. The participants in California who conceived of a teen this way listened to the teen's opinion but did not factor it into the decision unless they had additional evidence to endorse the teen's statement. If they did not, the teen's behaviour disqualified them from the status of participant. These study participants' negative views created a symbolic boundary between those youths who workers viewed as deserving of consultative participation versus collaborative or child-led participation. This was confirmed by the analysis conducted for Chapter 4: there were quite a few study participants in California (n=7) who viewed children, especially teens, negatively. When they mentioned teens who lied or manipulated their caseworkers or parents, the participants discussed situations when they did not deem the child's opinion significant. There was very little evidence of Norwegian workers labelling teenagers in this way – only one Norwegian worker thought so (and another worker mentioned a younger child as possibly lying). However, there was some evidence of positive labelling of children and negative labelling of parents in the Norwegian sample.

N19, the only Norwegian participant who, in response to the interview questions for this chapter, mentioned an adolescent who lied, discussed the case of an immigrant child from a low-income family who lied about his parents beating him because he thought he would have access to the consumer goods he wanted if he were moved into foster care. This is what N19 said:

'I also know that I've had children who lie, I know that, and I've tried to go into it with an adolescent, an immigrant youth who was placed after he said he was beaten, and it turned out not to be true ... Then the child moved back home, but it turned out that he thought that when you come to the child welfare services, then you get everything, clothing ... he came from a very impoverished family, an immigrant family, and he thought that when he was placed in a child welfare placement he'd suddenly get everything he wanted, brand-name clothing, etc.'

C11 said that children know how their families function and that workers should listen to them. She continued to say,

'So, if we listen to what they say, they can guide us. Every now and again, especially with teenagers, they're going to bend [the truth] to get what they want. And you have to be able to filter what they're saying to get [to the truth], because children, this is interesting about teenagers, it's interesting that around prom time, girls get in trouble, and they will scream, I'm being beaten, but nothing has happened, but they want to get out of the house, because they want to be able to go to the prom. So, you have to be able to filter what they're saying versus what's really going on.'

C39 was the worker who talked about the teenage girl who jumped out of the window of her parents' home and stated that her parents wanted to send her into an arranged marriage in the Middle East. She said that after talking with the family and other teenagers who knew the girl:

> '[I] found out that the kid had been basically trying to get her way and was trying to manipulate the family ... And then the kid's behaviour at the foster home: she was pissed because the foster parents wouldn't take her over the weekend to get her nails done, and she wanted all these videos to rent and stuff.'

The following quote by C15 shows that there are teens who do try to manipulate the system, which makes them untrustworthy. C15 was asked how she proceeded in cases where she disagreed with the child's opinion. She responded:

> 'Well, the only cases I can think of is unfortunate, where some teens are actively trying to get their parents in trouble. I do the same thing. I actively listen to the child and try to figure out what the main issues are, but there's more to what's going on than what's being said, but holistically, once again, we try to look at the big picture and try to figure out what's going on.'

This is how C40 labelled a child as able to manipulate the system:

> 'I have to say that children's ... opinion matters, but I also have to counterbalance [that] with their age or development and ... how long they've been in the system, because kids who have been in the system a long time, they get attorneys when we start off and if they're removed and so institutionalized children know how to manipulate the system.'

C40 then provided an example of a case in which a child's statement mattered much to her decision. Then she added, "but then also there are some kids who are trying to challenge authority, trying to subvert parental authority, and those cases, I hear them, but if they're just trying to have their way, I deal with them differently because it's not about protection; they're trying to get [one] over [their parents]".

C4 said when she replied to our question about how she proceeded when her opinion differed from that of the child she was working with:

'Well, again, it depends on the age … I'm probably more likely to get that from a teenager. And oftentimes it's like a narcissistic teenager who's like, you know, my parents are totally horrible, or whatever, and that's usually not exactly the situation. I try to redirect them to what role they play in it, and what responsibility they have in it. So, if it's a situation where I think it's pretty clear … that's why we're having a disagreement around it, and if it's around the child's behaviours … I do try to redirect it there and try to have them take some responsibility for it.'

C17 mentioned some of the behaviours of the teenagers she worked with that result in conflict with parents:

'It's important to listen to the child; even if the child lies to you, you need to listen to the lies very carefully as well. In other words, we have to take the child seriously when the child is talking to us. We cannot dismiss anything. That doesn't mean we're going to give the child what she wants, because that's what happens a lot here. We're filing [for a court order] on kids that we don't control all the time. There's no abuse. The abuse is only because the parents ask them, you need to go to school, you need to do some mild chores in the house, you cannot be going out with a 30-year-old man, you have to go to school daily though you don't want to, and you're not allowed to drink and come home drunk at 3:00 in the morning. And now you're saying, because I [parent] say this and that and yes, I might have slapped you, lost control, that [doesn't make me] an abuser. So, it's really challenging, very challenging.'

C16 was asked how she would determine whether a child was telling the truth or not in an investigation. She responded:

'Little kids, usually you could ask them if they know the difference between truth and lies. If I say "My pants are green, tell me what colour my pants are. Oh, you say they're brown? So, if I say they're green, is it truth or is it a lie?". Little kids may tell you things and not even realize what they're saying. Older kids … sometimes you ask if they have an agenda. How do you determine it? Sometimes

125

what other people are telling you, too. If a kid says, "Hey I'm doing really well in school". And then the teacher says, "Yeah. You got Ds and Fs. You're not doing really well in school." Investigations, we're all about child safety, but doing the investigation with the child, with the minor, is only a part of it. That's it.'

C6 stated that:

'if we feel like the child is telling us a story because … typically it might be a teenager where they want to get out of the house and so they're telling us a story to get out of the house; or they're telling us a story to get someone else out of the house. We just pretty much talk to them honestly and openly and tell them, "What you're telling us doesn't match what's going on, and we're not believing this, so what can we do to make this situation better?".'

C6 told us that if teenagers wanted to move out of their parents' home and she disagreed with that, she would "confront them with that":

'There are times when we tell the child, "We're not taking you away. You're going home." So sometimes we step in and act as the parent to the child, and tell them what their parents are not telling them, "You're going home, and you need to work this out with your parents because we're not going to step in. There's no reason for us to step in, so you need to go home".'

C17 viewed and approached teenagers in a similar manner. She said that "the truth behind the lies and the lies behind the truth" sometimes come out during a meeting. This is what she reported doing in meetings with teens who lie:

'So you've come to the table and you bring it up like it is, and you bring every single thing to [the table that] undermine what the kids say … And it's frustrating, all the truth, the lies … Yeah, and then it comes out. And then you recognize, make the family recognize, yes, I don't like it, although it's not inappropriate, but I don't like it because of my culture or because that's the way I was brought up and they let the kid hear that too. And say, recognize, yes, there is a problem and it's going to get worse unless there's this intervention. Now, can this intervention be done with the services ABC or what is going to happen? And I turn to the minor and I say, even though I hear you and all these things, and I know tomorrow if you get up in the morning you would like to change your life and you will have XYZ different than now, it's probably not going to happen [overnight]. There's a lot of work to do here and for better or for worse, these are your parents and you feel you want liberty? Let me tell you, you have liberty now. You have more liberty than you think. And I tell them, you know why, I said, because now let's assume that you go to Walgreen's and you steal, that's petty theft … And then your parents go and bail you out and you go home. Let's say that you are a substance abuser, they're not going to press charges because you're a minor, but when you're 18, you won't be able to do any of that. Because you know what? They're not going to call the child protection agency or call your parents; they're going to take you to jail. That's the choice you're making right now, I say. And really call it for what it is.'

Participants mentioned that when they suspected that a teen was manipulating them, they remained focused on gathering evidence to find out whether the teen's safety was endangered. One of them was C17, who said that in the case she described, where a teenage girl went out with a 30-year-old man and engaged in other risky behaviours, "it was important to get all the information as much as you can from the child, from the parents, from the school, even from their … friends, and then have the meeting after that". C17 described other teenage "high-risk behaviours": "they are sexually active; they don't use contraceptives; they're using drugs; they're experimenting with sex, drugs and high-risk behaviours like driving under the influence or getting into gang affiliations."

C19 recounted the case of a teenager who accused her mother, who had been violent to her in the past, of hitting her. C19 decided to move the girl to a temporary residence for adolescents while working with her mother around mental health and parenting issues. She scheduled mental health intake appointments for the teen and arranged for weekly meetings with the school counsellor and so on. This is how C19 explained her decision to convince the girl to move back home:

'But at this point when the case came in, the child doesn't have marks. There were no marks, no bruises, nothing. The child just says, "You know, she always threatens to hit me, she has hit me before", but it's just that day, and there are no marks. I mean, that's really hard to say, because we also have to take into consideration a lot of teenagers say that because they don't want to go home. So, is this true? We don't know. But there is a likelihood that it's true because in the past mum has done that. So, I had to convince the child to go back. She doesn't like it, she cried. And I said, "Let's give yourself a chance and give mum a chance to work at this. At least all of us can say we've tried." And just talking to her, she was open, and I said, "Then let's also try and do this. We should arrange with mum, once every two weekends you could go and spend the weekend with your auntie." Because she was, "I want to live with my auntie!". And we can say that, "Let's try this". And to mum, we'll be, "It's not every weekend, she will have, every other weekend she'll be home, and you can spend time with her. But every other weekend, let her have some family connection, spend time with auntie". And then it's also … important for the child to have the auntie's support, so if this falls apart, she has a place to go because auntie is already involved.'

C26 described a similar scenario:

'Well, a lot of times we are involved in cases where there's an adolescent minor who is having conflictual relations with their parents, and they will say that they don't feel safe, or they say that they don't want to return home, but in the investigation, we find that there is no substantial risk for them to be removed from the home. So therefore, a lot of times we'll have to have family meetings and explain to the child why the child protection agency is not going to step in and remove that child. Even though they say they don't want to return to the parent's home because they're not getting along or whatever, that's not necessarily a CPS matter, because there's not substantial risk in the home or substantial abuse … And that's actually quite common: you have a 17-year-old minor who's angry at their parents for some odd reason – whether they got punished or weren't allowed to go to a party, and they run away, and they say, "Well, I refuse to go home, because ...". You know, sometimes we really even think that they may make stuff up, but other times they just don't have a legitimate reason to not want to go home, just because they're mad at their parents. And that's not a child protection case.'

C22 stated:

'I don't believe that a kid should walk into a shelter and say, "I'm not going home because I'm being abused", and there's no proof of that. They're just upset because mum won't let them go out. I don't think we should listen to that. But I think if a kid comes to me and says, I'm being sexually abused, or I'm being beaten, I would tend to believe that because, you know, the details and the description, and clearly, they're upset.'

This is how C34 described how she dealt with false allegations in a meeting:

'And ... prior to us hearing [that the girl's allegations were false], us as a team – with the families and the professionals and the school – we had all felt that if these allegations were not true, that there was no reason for that child to be out of the home. And that there was just going to be a need to find a way how to talk to the youth, assuring her that she didn't have to fear being punished for making that false allegation. So what I did in this particular case, I stepped out of the main large meeting to speak with the youth and with her support person and pretty much told her that after we heard what she had said, that her family was in a position where they understand that she's going through a hard time in her life, that they're not giving up on her, and I just started sharing with her all the strengths that they had to say about her. And when she was hearing that, it's like her face started to glow, you know, and then I just basically told her, "Our position from our agency is ... we have every right to make a decision if you're not going to be safe in your home, to place you out of that home, but in this situation that's not the case". And in acknowledging how she was feeling, that tell me if I'm wrong, tell me that you're afraid that you might be punished. And she said, "Yeah". So, after going through all of that conversation she then was able to say, "I'm okay to go back home". And the next thing she hugged me and then we went back and then the family, you know, approached her and hugged. And, so it was a very, very positive outcome of the meeting. But it started off where we all thought, well can it be true, these allegations that she's saying? And, that's how it came out.'

The study participants who perceived teens as lying to manipulate the situation in their favour still listened to and consulted with teens, but they did not appear to take their opinions and wishes seriously, unless they found evidence corroborating the teens' account.

Conclusion

In this book, I conceptualize citizenship as the status of a person who is recognized (formally, through legislation, and in interactions with others) as someone who holds the power to participate in decisions. There is strong evidence in the data of age serving as a symbolic boundary between a child's genuine participation (being consulted *and* empowered) and being consulted but not given power. The research participants in this study described their interactions with teenagers as providing participatory opportunities for them. The ways in which the study participants described their interactions with teens showed that they accepted their status as citizens. They reported listening to and consulting teens more so than younger children. They stated that they involved teens earlier and more directly in an investigation by speaking with them or meeting with them separately from their parents, by inviting them to meetings, and by communicating with them more honestly about the problems they saw in a case.

While teens' participation level was reportedly higher than that of younger children, the way in which the participants perceived teens affected the degree to which workers let them participate. Several study participants in both countries described some teenagers as defiant, rebellious, and resistant to interventions. These teens were perceived as more able and likely to undermine an effective intervention of the child protection agency, for instance, by running away or resisting the child protection agency's decision(s) in another way. This conceptualization of teenagers (as defiant) did sometimes, but not always, allow for collaborative and child-led participation.

The data showed that quite a few of the participants in California depicted some teenagers as liars and manipulators of their parents and the child protection system. These negative depictions of teens carry connotations of moral failure. The study participants consulted with these teens, but collaborative participation was out of the question because the participants focused on finding out the truth about the teens' situation to assess the risk to the teen. If the study participants had other evidence backing up what these teens were saying, collaborative participation seemed possible.

I was puzzled by this depiction of teens by experienced child protection caseworkers who were supportive of young people's participation (in theory and practice). It could very well be that the Californian participants were more concerned and/or thought more about lying teens because of their child protection system's focus on protection through risk assessment in investigations rather than preventive services as in Norway.[1] In a child protection system that is focused on assessing risk once a report of maltreatment has been screened in (rather than preventing maltreatment through parental guidance and public services in the early stages of a case as the Norwegian system does), investigators must attempt to assess the child's situation in a short time frame. In this context, figuring out the truth about a child's situation is especially important because the work of assessing risk requires truthful evidence. Given the context in which they practise, it is understandable that child protection caseworkers in California were more concerned about "telling the truth from the lies".

Piper's (2008) research on the cultural constructions of children in *Youth Matters: Next Steps* (a consultation document published by the UK Department for Education and Skills (2005)) is instructive when it comes to the construction of children's citizenship in the interactions with child protection caseworkers. Piper found four types of constructs of children in the document: the child as victim, as threat, as current citizen, especially as consumer–citizen, and as future productive citizen. I detected the teen as consumer–citizen (as exemplified in the quote by N19) and the teen as future productive citizen (as seen in the quote by C17). The data used for this chapter suggest another construct – that of youths as citizens. The study participants drew a symbolic participation boundary between younger children and teens. Many of them typically described teens as powerful – as defiant and rebellious. They viewed and treated them as participants by consulting with them or working with them (collaborative participation).

7

Protecting children, creating citizens

At the beginning of the journey that became this book, I set out to learn how child protection caseworkers help create the conditions for children's citizenship through their interactions with children, young people and their families. Child protection caseworkers are in a particularly important position to help children and young people who encounter the child protection system achieve citizenship status by promoting their participation. As the 'street-level bureaucrats' (Lipsky, 1980) implementing child welfare policy on the frontlines of child protection, the ways in which child protection caseworkers interact with children and young people on a regular basis can promote or stifle children's participation. I have shown here that many of the child protection caseworkers I studied created citizens in their interactions with children and young people while seeking to protect them from harm.

I asked a number of questions. First, given children's growing status,[1] how do the professionals working in child protection agencies[2] empower children by promoting their participation in important decisions when they investigate child maltreatment and provide support services to children and families? A child's genuine participation occurs when children are informed, able to reflect, develop and express their own opinions. Children's opinions and wishes are then considered in the decisions during investigations, removal from home, out-of-home placements, contact with parents, choice of schools, extracurricular activities, and other related decisions. Do professionals give children the opportunity to reflect on what is going on in their lives and develop opinions about what should happen? Do they listen to children's wishes and take them seriously? Which beliefs about children and young people do child protection workers draw on that influence the extent to which they promote children's participation? What are the effects of policy and organizational factors, such as practice guidelines and approaches, on workers' participatory practices? The aim of answering these questions was to contribute to the existing knowledge base about children's participation in child protection by showing the participatory approaches that exist in child protection practice.

Citizens are people who actively participate in decisions about their lives and the communities in which they live. If child protection caseworkers promote children's participation in these decisions, they also play a role in promoting their status as citizens. Of course, children's interactions with other children and young people and other adults may contribute to children's and young people's status as citizens as well. For the purpose of this book, I zoomed in on the role of child protection professionals. The participation of children in child protection-related decisions is only one 'building block' – to use a term borrowed from Lister (2008) – of a larger historical trajectory towards children's citizenship and children's rights. Nonetheless, it is worthy of exploration because abused and neglected children are in an especially vulnerable position. These children's citizenship is not only opposed by cultural narratives and practices of adult-centrism, but by ableism, classism, homophobia, xenophobia, and racism. We know that youth with disabilities constituted 31.8 per cent of the entire foster care population in the US in 2012 (Slayter, 2016). We also know that children from lower socioeconomic backgrounds are at higher risk of maltreatment in the US (Cancian et al, 2010; Berger et al, 2013; Eckenrode et al, 2014), and children of colour are overrepresented among children in care (US Department of Health and Human Services. Children's Bureau, 2018). In Norway, a higher proportion of immigrant children and adolescents (0–22 years) receive child protection measures (Statistics Norway, 2015).

Children's substantive citizenship is a relational concept of meaning and practice. It comes to life in interactions between human beings who communicate and interact with each other. They bring their experiences, views, and values about the world to their interactions. I leaned on the symbolic interactionist theoretical tradition and especially West and Zimmerman's work of 'doing gender' (West and Zimmerman, 1987) for my study. I drew on this theoretical platform to propose the concept of 'doing participation' to delineate how citizenship is accomplished through interactions between children and child protection caseworkers. I further employed Lamont and Molnar's (2002) idea of 'symbolic boundaries' to analyze how child protection workers' classifications of children, especially in terms of age, affect the extent to which they do participation.

The book rests on empirical data gathered in Norway and the US and prior scholarship on the topic. I analyzed a total of 68 qualitative interviews conducted with child protection workers in Norway (n=28) and in California in the US (n=40). I focused on workers' experiences, views and organizational contexts because previous research on children's involvement in child protection-related processes has shown that it is important to consider organizational factors, such as the procedures employed by a child protection agency, to understand the extent to which children's participation occurs in child protection (Vis et al, 2012; Vis and Fossum, 2013; Vis and Fossum, 2015). Research suggests that organizational practices, the social norms underpinning organizations in the child protection system, and workers' skills and attitudes affect how and to what extent children participate (Vis and Fossum, 2013; Vis and Fossum, 2015).

In the following, I shall first describe the participation boundaries reported by the child protection caseworkers in this study before discussing the ways in which they do participation.

Participation boundaries

The child protection workers interviewed for this study in Norway and the US (California) reported situations in which they thought they could, or would not, involve children. Workers reported not involving children when they were too young to understand what was happening or could not verbalize their feelings or opinions. The study participants did not involve a child to avoid running the risk of a child facing their abuser in person in a meeting or of distressing or retraumatizing the child in other ways. This points to protective attitudes among child protection workers, which have been documented by prior research (Sanders and Mace, 2006; Vis et al, 2012). A few participants mentioned that they would not involve children if children did not want to be involved. The participants mentioned not involving children who were incapacitated by a physical disability or mental illness. This finding points to the importance of studying participation from an intersectional perspective (Crenshaw, 1989; Collins, 1993) – a view recently proposed by Petersen (Petersen, 2018). An intersectional paradigm considers that child protection caseworkers' ways of treating children may differ by a child's social position – their class, gender, nation, race/ethnicity, ability, age and sexuality. Recent research about the experience of immigrant youth in Norway by Knag Fylkesnes et al (2018) also evidences the importance of analyzing children's participation from such a perspective. The authors, who interviewed six young people of colour of migrant background involved in the child protection system, found that children experienced participation as well as 'ambiguous participation' and non-participation. This research showed that assimilatory cultural forces may adversely affect the agency and participation of young people of colour whose parents immigrated to Norway:

> embedded cultural ideas of 'how children should act' emerged as a potential barrier for participation, silencing youth's everyday experiences and wishes. Youth with ethnic minority backgrounds, whose identities might be at odds with prevailing norms, may therefore struggle to make themselves accountable within the structural arrangements of CWS [Child Welfare Services]. (Knag Fylkesnes et al, 2018, p 346)

Future research will need to analyze more systematically how children's age, gender, social class, sexuality, disabilities, race, and ethnicity affect the extent to which and how child protection caseworkers promote their participation.

The protection boundary

Where did the study participants draw the line between promoting children's participation and non-participation? Participants reported not involving children in situations where they thought children's involvement would distress or retraumatize them. They avoided children meeting with their abuser in cases of physical and sexual abuse (as reported in California). If children felt intimidated by their interactions with the child protection system, the participants would ask them to choose a spokesperson as an intermediary (as mentioned in Norway). Study participants stated that they made decisions for children to protect them from loyalty conflicts and feelings of guilt, for example, when children preferred one parent over the other in custody battles.

The protection principle prevailed over children's genuine participation when the child's safety was at risk. Workers in both countries reported not letting children make decisions when the risk of harm to the child was imminent and serious, especially in cases of sexual and physical abuse. Time and again, the study participants stressed that they would decide against a child's wishes in situations where they thought that the child's choice would not be safe. This echoes the findings of Vis et al (2012), which highlight child protection workers' protective attitude as a barrier to children's participation. Several participants mentioned that the time-sensitivity of serious cases, where a child is in imminent danger and needs to be removed from home quickly, precludes a child's involvement in decision-making. The stage of a case in combination with the level of risk to the child defines the protection boundary. During the investigation stage into child maltreatment, the tension between children's protection and participation is particularly high, and tilted towards protection. The choices that children are consulted about are very narrow in these situations. Workers may give children choices about how and to what degree they want to be involved. They may ask them about wishes for their placements or extracurricular activities once children have been placed. The decision about removal clearly rests with child protection workers. This finding resonates with children's experiences with removal situations reported by Balsells et al (2017) for Spain, and Križ and Roundtree-Swain (2017) for the north-eastern US, where children reported not having any input into removal situations. The danger of imminent risk was also identified as a participation barrier in Vis and Thomas' (2009) study of case managers in Norway, and the review of scholarship on children's participation in child protection (in the Global North) by van Bijleveld et al (2014).

The age, ability and vulnerability boundaries

Two age-related boundaries emerged from the data: an involvement boundary related to a child's young age (infancy up to the age of four years versus older children) as a result of young children's perceived lower levels of understanding and ability to articulate. The second participation boundary involved pre-teens and teens versus younger children. Workers in both countries tried to overcome the young age boundary by providing age-appropriate information to very young children, and by assessing the risk to them in other ways than involving them directly. The age boundaries were conceptualized differently by the California and Norwegian study participants. The participants in California who mentioned young age as a non-involvement trigger either thought that young children were too vulnerable to be exposed to information related to physical and sexual abuse or that workers could not gather information or evidence from young children by speaking with them during an investigation, because young children were either pre-verbal or too young to understand what was happening. Norwegian workers were as likely as Californian workers to perceive the young age boundary, but they did not link young age to vulnerability, as some of the Californian workers did. A few of the Norwegian workers depicted young children as knowledgeable about what is occurring in their family. As a group, the Norwegian workers were less likely to mention emotional distress or traumatization as reasons not to involve children.

This could reflect cultural differences in views about young children in Norway and the US, or the differences in the severity of the cases of the sample of participants in Norway and California. The study participants in California were recruited in emergency response units. These units assess the risk to the child after a referral of child maltreatment has been screened in for investigation by the agency and therefore these participants had to make decisions in situations of great urgency. In addition, the intervention threshold is higher in California than in Norway (Skivenes and Stenberg, 2015; Skivenes and Søvig, 2017). Many study participants emphasized that a child's ability to clearly, strongly and/or credibly communicate their feelings, opinions and wishes, either verbally or non-verbally (through physical reactions or by acting out, for example), led them to take the child seriously.

Doing participation

Almost half of the research participants in this study (31 out of 68) reported facilitating children's participation by consulting with children and considering their opinions and wishes when making decisions. They did so in the following ways: they actively engaged children, learned about them and their lives, and sought their trust. They provided information that allowed children to understand what was going on with their case, form their own opinions and make informed decisions. They gave children time and space to express their opinions. They also divested power away from themselves and towards children through a type of presentation of self I have called 'recognition work': they presented themselves to children in a way that conveyed that they recognized children's feelings and wishes and saw them as valuable contributors to a decision. Finally, workers promoted 'youth citizens' by including pre-teens and teens as consultants and collaborators in important decisions.

Engaging children and building trust

Sociologists have long theorized the importance of trust in building and maintaining social relationships. The 19th century French sociologist Emile Durkheim, in response to liberal (individualistic) economic thought at the time, argued that human beings must establish mutual trust to engage in beneficial economic exchanges (Collins and Makowsky, 2009). My study revealed that children's participation can be achieved when workers engage children and gain their trust by asking questions, when they attempt to learn about them and actively listen to them. As my findings on workers' perceptions of children show, their trust in children is important in their willingness to do participation. The process of establishing mutual trust between children and their caseworkers takes time and communication. These findings support prior studies that showed the importance of a respectful, trusting relationship between children and child protection workers in fostering children's participation (Festinger, 1983; Bell, 2002; Smith et al, 2003; Healy and Darlington, 2009; Vis et al, 2012; Cossar et al, 2014; Eidhammer, 2014; Burford and Gallagher, 2015; Paulsen, 2015, 2016; Nord Sæbjørnsen and Willumsen, 2017).

Dahlø Husby et al (2018) interviewed ten children aged nine to 17 years of Norwegian ethnic background who were in contact with child welfare services in Norway about how they experience collaboration with professionals in meetings and how professionals facilitate children's participation. The researchers found that children had a wide range of experiences with participation. Professionals' careful listening, emotional support through verbal and non-verbal communication, access to tools that encourage play and games, professionals who showed interest in children's feelings, understanding and empathy and recognized the child, and trusting relationships were perceived by the children as essential to promoting participation (Dahlø Husby et al, 2018).

The importance of children's trust as a stepping stone towards participation has been emphasized by the young people in The Change Factory, which works for institutional change in the education, child protection, healthcare and justice systems in Norway. The Change Factory's 'pros' underscore that trust is the basis of successful communication. If children do not trust adults, they will not feel safe, and they will not be honest with adults (Forandringsfabrikken, 2018b). Soerlie's (2018) case study of child protection investigations in five Norwegian child welfare offices examined how child protection agencies can foster children's participation during investigations. The children interviewed insisted that it was crucial that child protection caseworkers cared for them, and that children experienced them as trustworthy. Families' views of child protection services, which are influenced by (negative) reports in the media, can adversely affect children's and parents' participation. Workers need to address children's and families' negative views before children can trust them (Soerlie, 2018).

I learned about the work of The Change Factory (*Forandringsfabrikken*) at a conference in Bergen, Norway, in summer 2018. The Change Factory consists of a group of young people who had been in care who seek to improve the Norwegian child protection system based on children's experiences. For over 15 years they have worked tirelessly towards changing laws and practice guidelines. Their aim is to create child protection agencies, schools, healthcare institutions, police departments and courts that are safe and useful for children (Barnevernsproffene, 2011; Forandringsfabrikken, 2018a, 2018b). The efforts of The Change Factory's 'pros' – the children and young people who are active in this movement – are remarkable and reflect the rising social status of children in societies of the Global North (Zelizer, 1994; James and Prout, 1997). When Fredrik and Glorija, two of the pros active with The Change Factory, talked about their work, the audience was captivated. Glorija explained that the basis of children's participation in decision-making in child protection must be love: children need to feel that professionals care about them, so they can feel safe and be honest with adults. In fact, one of The Change Factory's accomplishments has been the inclusion of the word 'love' as a guiding principle in child protection law in Norway (Forandringsfabrikken, 2018a, 2018b).

Providing information to children

Sixty per cent of the study participants (41 out of 68) reported providing information to children in the child protection process. The information they provided in meetings was about the workers' responsibility, the role of the agency and the availability of a spokesperson for the child (as is the case in Norway). This type of information can be crucial to ensuring children's participation because it allows children to reflect on what is happening and develop an opinion. This is especially important in removal situations. Prior research has shown that children often lack information about the reasons for their removal and the removal process (Festinger, 1983; Hochman et al, 2004; Eidhammer, 2014; Burford and Gallagher, 2015; Balsells et al, 2017; Križ and Roundtree-Swain, 2017; Knag Fylkesnes et al, 2018).

Many of the child protection caseworkers in this study explained the reasons behind the decisions they had made and delineated who had been responsible for making the decision. The extent to which workers' provision of information *to* children was paired with consulting *with* children depended on the stage of a case. Caseworkers involved in emergency investigations must assess the risk to the child in a swift manner and are focused on gathering, rather than giving, information. The information that investigating workers provided to children during investigations tended to be logistical (about what was happening, what the worker was doing, who made the decisions), rather than empowering.

It takes communication skills, time and energy on the part of child protection workers to explain agency rationales and decisions, especially in a situation where the agency's decision runs counter to children's wishes. Examples include: when children want to return home, but workers think it is in their best interest to remain in foster care; when children do not want to return home, but workers determine no substantial risk and decide children need to return home; or, when children refuse a support measure that workers deem necessary. A recent research review by ten Brummelaar, Harder, Kalverboer, Post and Knorth (2017) on youth in residential care in the Netherlands found that professionals' positive views of young people and their skills in fostering participation in interactions with children are pivotal to children's participation, as this book has shown.

Giving children time and space to communicate

Workers who conducted child protection investigations were primarily focused on gathering information to determine the level of risk to the child. These workers, too, spent time with children to learn about their lives and their family's strengths when talking with them during home visits. They took the time and gave children the space to talk about their families and express their opinions and wishes. Children feel more inclined to express their opinions and wishes when child protection workers gain children's trust (and vice versa) and provide communicative space. Organizational practices that allowed children to voice their thoughts in a safe space were mentioned as springboards towards children's participation. Tools that helped engage children, such as 'The River of Life' in Norway, allowed workers to get to know children and their family in a structured way. In California, TDMs gave children the chance to tell their story and express their wishes and opinions. However, it seems that children were not consistently invited to TDMs, especially when they were younger, or when workers thought that their participation would retraumatize them.

Divesting power through recognition work

Child protection workers must often make decisions that run counter to children's wishes in order to protect them. When this happened, the study participants reported signalling to children that they understood their feelings and acknowledged their wishes, even if they disagreed with what they wanted. Several of the participants mentioned being clear and honest with children. These may have been their ways of showing respect and recognizing children's opinions. These workers sought to convey to children that they took their opinions seriously (even if they ultimately did not go along with them) by empathizing and respecting their feelings and views. I have called this approach 'recognition work', in reference to a similar strategy to divesting power that Križ et al (2012) found among child protection workers in the north-eastern US. These workers engaged in 'status and dignity work' when practising with non-citizen immigrant children, youth and families. They acknowledged immigrant parents' wishes for their children in this approach. They emphasized their strengths as parents, thus signalling respect and divesting power to parents. Similarly, Soerlie (2018) suggests that caseworkers need to maintain a family's dignity during child protection investigations by discussing the strengths as well as the deficiencies present in the family. Ten Brummelaar et al (2016), who studied children's participation in residential care in the Netherlands, found a similar type of power divestment approach among social workers employed in residential care institutions in the Netherlands. The authors quoted one of the workers as saying, 'in this I also use myself as a subject, being vulnerable, belittling myself in front of the boys. Simply being approachable. I am no more than they are. I just try to help them' (ten Brummelaar et al (2016), p 700). Several of the study participants interviewed for this book, too, shifted power towards children or at least told children that they were trying to do so.

Creating youth citizens

Most study participants distinguished between teenagers and younger children. Youth – seen as children older than 12 years by the study participants – were considered by many of the participants as more powerful than younger children. They were believed to possess the ability to actively and successfully resist the child protection agency's decisions and interventions. Several participants in California and Norway described teens as defiant, rebellious, and able to resist agency interventions. The teens' defiant behaviour influenced the workers' decisions and the teens got what they wished in some situations. This finding echoes the study of Križ and Roundtree-Swain (2017). It showed that teens can affect the decision taken by the child protection agency when they strongly advocate for their wishes (verbally or through their actions). In other instances, the teens' resistance and advocacy can be futile. Future research will need to further determine the situations in which teens' advocacy skills effectively impact workers' decisions.

Most of the study participants talked about children 12 years and older when they described situations in which children's opinion mattered to their decision. None of them mentioned a case in which a child was younger than five years. Many of the participants explicitly stated that they heavily weighed the opinions of teens (and, less frequently, pre-teens) because of their age. The conception of teens as inherently more powerful and less controllable than younger children affected how workers did participation. A few participants in Norway reported meeting and talking with teens earlier in an investigation. Teens were offered more substantial choices and given the opportunity to develop their own options. Workers reported communicating with teens in a more honest and straightforward way in meetings about their options and decisions, including decisions about out-of-home placements. (Some participants encouraged teens' participation, while others viewed them negatively and did not take their opinions seriously, as discussed in Chapter 5).

Roads to children's participation in child protection

The literature on children's decision-making has provided concrete suggestions for steps towards change in child protection. These steps are crucial in granting children the right to develop and express their opinions and to ensure that their voices are heard and taken seriously. Here are a few examples. Skivenes and Strandbu (2006) outlined four mechanisms that may lead to the participation of children. First, children must have the opportunity to develop their own opinions. They need to have the information to develop a viewpoint, reflect on and be informed about the consequences of the decision. Second, children must be able to express their opinions in decision-making processes, either by speaking themselves or having a trusted spokesperson speak on their behalf. Third, children's arguments must be included in the deliberations about a decision; a spokesperson may need to be appointed to ensure that children's viewpoints are heard. Fourth, there needs to be follow-up to a decision: children must receive information about how a decision has been reached, what the results mean, and how a decision can be appealed. They must have the opportunity to ask questions. Lastly, the decision-making processes must be controlled by an external entity to minimize the abuse of power

(Skivenes and Strandbu, 2006). Norwegian researchers Vis and Fossum (2015) call for more clarity in rules and procedures to deal with the variation in organizational cultures and attitudes of professionals: 'It is our belief that leaders and policy-makers should address differences in culture and decision-making practices in Child Protective Services with clearer standards and regulations about when and how children are to be involved in care planning' (p 284).

Archard and Skivenes (2009b) consider the following necessary to facilitate children's participation: children need to be informed about the issues they are involved in, need to be able to ask questions, and must have the time and space to reflect on the issues so they can develop their own opinion. Children will be more likely to present their views in an environment that is child-friendly, and in which they feel comfortable, for instance, in surroundings that they are used to from their everyday lives. Participation takes time and trust, which cannot be built in one single meeting between children and adults. Children may feel intimidated in the presence of an adult. It may therefore be easier for children if the presence of adults is minimized or a spokesperson represents children's wishes if they are not confident enough to express them. Adults need to explain to children what role their views played in the decision that was ultimately made. Children's maturity should be assessed independently of the decision about what is in their best interest. Archard and Skivenes (2009b) stated that 'most importantly, and as an overarching rule, we think that it violates a principle of equity to require the child to display a level of maturity that it would be unreasonable to expect of most competent adults' (p 394).

Innovative initiatives, programmes and practice tools seeking to empower children and young people in child protection initiated by non-governmental organizations and researchers in the field have recently emerged in all parts of the globe, sometimes in collaboration with public child protection agencies. Researchers Heggdalsvik and Barmen Tysnes initiated an innovative research-based development project together with their undergraduate social work students in collaboration with the municipality of Bergen, Norway. They developed an online, evidence-based tool for child protection workers, so they can elicit and document children's voices in investigations and when undertaking support measures. When caseworkers open their computer program, they now fill out a form that prompts them to answer several questions, such as 'What information has been given to the child?'. The form includes five sections: background information about the child, the objective of the conversation, information about the conversation with the child, a summary of the conversation, and the caseworker's assessment of the child's situation after the conversation. A preliminary evaluation of the tool has shown that it has helped caseworkers plan their conversations with children (Heggdalsvik and Barmen Tysnes, 2018).

The young people from The Change Factory in Norway have asked professionals to embrace the following values and attitudes when working with children and young people: be open and honest with children and provide good and enough information; show love by sharing warmth, in your body (eyes) and with your words; create a safe environment by, for example, providing information about yourself to children; and, be humble – believe in children, listen with the purpose to understand, and apologize. The Change Factory's pros argue that, when children feel safe, they will be more honest with child protection workers. This, in turn, will boost the child protection system's efficiency by rendering children safer more quickly (Forandringsfabrikken, 2018b). In California, the California Youth Connection has been instrumental in lobbying for legislative change for foster youth since 1988. One of their most prominent accomplishments is the 2001 Foster Youth Bill of Rights (California Youth Connection, 2020).

Researchers in Spain have developed and implemented an arts-based approach to promote children's participation in programme evaluation. Children aged six to 12 years in families at risk of poverty and social disadvantage draw their experiences with a family support program and discuss them in small groups with the help of an adult researcher-facilitator. Children experience the impact of the group sessions as empowering, and their voices act as catalysts for parental change (Fuentes-Peláez et al, 2018). Researchers in Denmark have worked with immigrant youth in residential care units in a project called BELLA. The young people in this project (aged 14–17 years) acted as co-researchers and agents of change in their local community. Through this partnership, the young people gained confidence, as expressed by this participant:

> We have become very brave. We stood up in front of a lot of people and did something we never knew we could do. We had a great experience. We travelled to another country to get the chance to tell about our project … It was cool to come as young people and teach the adults something. (Quoted in Petersen, 2018)

The Making My History project with children and young people in residential care homes in Brazil seeks to empower children so they can take charge of their own life stories and present themselves and their views in interactions with institutions such as the courts. The initiative has reached almost 14,000 children since 2005. Children work on their life stories with a volunteer at their residential centre in weekly meetings throughout their care trajectory. Thus, they can establish strong bonds with an adult by producing an album about their life story. Children include their life experiences in the album, including their experiences of removal from home and their experiences in residential care. Children have used various methods to tell their stories (a newspaper, a book and videos) and presented their work at an exhibit in the Sao Paolo courthouse. This project has increased children's self-confidence, skills and sense of control, promoted their protection and improved decision-making (Naddeo and Vidiz, 2018).

There have also been interesting theoretical developments regarding children's participation in child protection. For example, Mimi Petersen has combined the theory of recognition by Honneth (1996), the theory of intersectionality (Crenshaw, 1989; Collins, 1993) and the *protagonismo infantil* approach with Hart's ladder of participation (Hart, 1992) (see Petersen, 2018). This kind of theoretical synthesis will allow scholars of children's participation to widen the scope of future inquiries into children's participation in child protection. The theory of intersectionality (Collins, 1993) draws attention to 'the matrix of domination' that affects individuals differently according to their social position and operates at the institutional levels (through educational and governmental institutions, for example), the symbolic level (through oppressive images and language), and at the individual levels, affecting individual biographies. *Protagonismo infantil* is an action-oriented paradigm stemming from Latin America in the 1960s. It describes the agency of child labourers and other exploited children to resist social oppression and recognizes that children's agency needs to be supported by all sectors of a community (Alfageme et al, 2003). The term is more encompassing than 'children's participation' as it is used here because it calls for a restructuring of society as a whole (Gaytá, 1998).

Conclusion

The aim of this book was to show in what ways child protection caseworkers employed by public child protection agencies in Norway and California create citizens by promoting the participation of children and young people in their interactions with them. Citizens are understood as people who can make decisions about their lives and the communities in which they live. I argued that child protection professionals play a role in creating citizens by promoting children's and young people's participation in important decisions that affect their lives. While there are many formidable barriers to children's and young people's participation in child protection, as I showed based on prior research in Chapter 2 and my own data material in Chapter 4, my findings demonstrated that there is a group of child protection caseworkers who promote the participation of children and young people in various ways. Chapters 5, 6 and 7 discussed the ways in which the child protection caseworkers in my study promoted children's and young people's participation in child protection-related processes. My hope is that research on the participatory views, knowledge, skills and practices of child protection caseworkers will continue in the future to highlight how these professionals can play a salient role in creating children's citizenship.

APPENDIX 1

Research methods

The analysis I undertook for this book was part of a larger, ten-year, mixed-methods research project entitled CHILDPRO, which compared the child protection systems of England, Norway, and the US between 2007 and 2017. The project was funded by the Norwegian Research Council and managed by Marit Skivenes, Professor at the University of Bergen (UiB), Norway, and director of the Centre for Research on Discretion and Paternalism at UiB. We selected these countries because they represent different types of child welfare systems (Gilbert et al, 2011). The research sites within each country were largely chosen for practical considerations, especially accessibility.

For this book, I used a portion of the qualitative data material we gathered in Norway and the US. The aim of the qualitative interviews was to learn how child protection workers in the three countries viewed children's participation, experienced their collaboration with the police and courts, undertook practice with immigrant children, youth and families, and thought of their respective country's child protection policies. The project, including the ethics procedures, was vetted by the ombudsman for research with human subjects in Norway. The study was peer-reviewed during the funding application process in Norway.

Data collection

Dr Marit Skivenes, the principal investigator for the project, recruited the study participants by approaching two municipalities in Norway and child welfare agencies in two cities in California. In Norway, the research was conducted in Sandefjord and Stavanger between January and March 2008. In each municipality, Dr Skivenes interviewed 14 participants. (The towns allowed the project to identify their names in publications. The interview transcripts were de-identified in other ways before analyses were conducted.) In Norway, the municipalities provided the project with email addresses of social workers employed by the respective municipality. Dr Skivenes sent out an invitation email to all the workers in the agency, including those who conducted investigations at the front end of cases and those responsible for providing ongoing services. The research in the US was carried out in two cities in California. The heads of the child protection agencies in the two cities were approached about participating in the study. They emailed an invitation letter to all the social workers and supervisors working in their emergency response units. The letter explained the project, stated that participation in the study was voluntary and discussed the implications of the study. The workers who were interested in participating contacted Dr Skivenes by email or phone. Dr Skivenes conducted the 24 interviews in Norway and most of the interviews in California. I conducted 16 interviews in California between March and June 2010. Most of the interviews were conducted face-to-face, with a few over the phone. All happened during non-work hours, lasted between one and 1.5 hours and were digitally recorded and transcribed verbatim (into English and Norwegian). We chose interview locations that were convenient for the participants, including meeting rooms and public places. The study participants provided informed consent before the interviews commenced. Study participants received an honorarium of $150 for their participation in the interview and for answering an online survey. In the publications for the project, we de-identified the data by using female pronouns for all the participants and assigning code numbers to the participants.

The sample

The samples from both countries consisted of very experienced and mostly female social workers employed by public child protection agencies working face-to-face with children, youth, and families. The Californian sample was more experienced than the Norwegian one: on average, the study participants in California had 16 years of work experience. (The variance was 28 years.) Their median work experience amounted to 15 years. In California overall, social workers and supervisors worked an average of 11.3 years in child protection in 2011 (California Social Work Education Center, 2011). The average work experience of the Norwegian sample was 10 years (the variance was 33 years), with a median experience of 8 years. In both countries, several participants were managers or supervisors with a wide range of experience in the field of child protection (as investigators as well as ongoing workers). In California, caseworkers were recruited in emergency response units. These are units in which workers undertake risk assessments following referrals to a phone hotline which have been screened in for assessment. Workers in these units assess the risk to a child expeditiously – within 10 days after the referral was screened in, or within two hours if the child is in imminent danger (Reed and Karpilow, 2002; Berrick Duerr et al, 2015b). If the case is substantiated, the child will either be removed from home or voluntary services will be provided. In the latter case, the emergency response units can provide services for up to 30 days (Reed and Karpilow, 2002). The Norwegian study participants were more evenly divided between investigating workers and those providing ongoing services. The participants were almost all white and did not belong to an ethnic minority group in Norway. The Californian sample was more ethnically and racially diverse. While the exact breakdown in terms of participants' ethnic and racial background is not known, the data on ethnic and racial background from the survey responses gathered in the same Californian agencies from which we recruited the interview participants indicated the extent of participants' racial/ethnic diversity: 24 of the 52 survey participants who answered the question on ethnic and racial background self-identified as a person of colour. If the ethnic and racial background of the participants for this study was roughly the same, the Californian sample appears to reflect the ethnic and racial diversity of the child protective workforce in California: in 2011, 14 per cent of public child protection workers in California identified as Hispanic/Latino(a), 10.7 per cent as Mexican American, 9.9 per cent as African American, 5 per cent as Asian American, 4.5 per cent as biracial/ethnic, 2.3 per cent as multiracial/ethnic, 0.9 per cent as American Indian, and 51.6 per cent as White (California Social Work Education Center, 2011).

The Californian sample was more educated. All Norwegian study participants but one, who had a master's degree, had earned a bachelor's degree. In California most of the participants held a graduate degree: 27 had earned a master's degree and two a PhD. Only one worker held a bachelor's degree. In the state of California in 2011, 60 per cent of public child protection workers held a master's degree of some kind; 40 per cent of these held a master's degree in social work (California Social Work Education Center, 2011). The high proportion of workers with graduate degrees in the Californian sample was the result of the specific hiring pattern in one of the agencies in California, which only hired staff with a master's degree. The skew towards a very highly educated and senior sample was also caused by the economic recession: when we interviewed in California, we heard that many of the junior-level caseworkers had been dismissed because of budget cuts related to the recession. According to a report on the Californian child protective services from 2011, California's 58 counties overall lost 10.7 per cent of their child welfare workers and supervisors between 2008 and 2011. There were 21.4 per cent fewer caseload carrying child welfare workers and 7.2 per cent fewer supervisors in 2011 than in 2008 (California Social Work Education Center, 2011). According to the California Social Work Education Center, '[s]tatewide, 47 counties reported that 401 child welfare staff positions were not filled in 2010–2011 due to concern about the economy. Additionally, 12 counties anticipated losing positions in 2011–2012 and 42 counties laid off 33 staff in 2010–2011' (California Social Work Education Center, 2012, p 1). The Californian sample is not representative of the child welfare workforce in the US overall. Almost half of child protection workers in the US did not hold a bachelor's degree in social work, and slightly under 40 per cent of workers have a bachelor's or master's degree in social work (Barth et al, 2008).

Data material and analyses

I used the data from in-depth, semi-structured interviews with 28 social workers employed by two municipalities in Norway and with 40 social workers employed by public child protection agencies in California. I translated the Norwegian data into English with the help of a translation software. (I am a native German speaker who knows Swedish, so I can read Norwegian fairly well.) Subsequently, a (native Norwegian) research assistant employed by the CHILDPRO project reviewed my translations for accuracy. I employed standard qualitative data analysis techniques to analyze the data (see Weiss, 1994 and Lofland et al, 2006). First, I read the interview responses to determine the themes that emerged from the data. In a second step, I reread the responses to detect the common denominators of these themes by comparing them with other themes. After I had decided on the overarching codes, I coded the material using the software program Atlas.ti. I ran a word count through Atlas.ti and calculated the frequencies of the codes to check for analytical biases (Maxwell, 2005). I presented as many quotations from the interviews as possible to check for biases in my analysis and presentation of the data.

I shall, in what follows, describe the interview questions I used and the codes that emerged from the data.

Table A.1: Code descriptions for Chapter 3

Code	Content
Ability	Children's developmental delays; suicidality; mental illness (depression, schizophrenia) and physical or mental disability, such as speech problems, physical injury to the head, or autism; children do not have the capacity to understand.
Age	Involvement depends on the child's age; children are too young to understand and to articulate what happened or give their opinion, or they are too young to be involved in meetings where abuse is being discussed; strategies to involve children despite their young age.
Impact	Children should not be involved in investigations or review meetings because they may be intimidated, stressed or retraumatized; providing children with information (or details of a case) or putting them between their parents in parental conflict or custody battles would burden or frighten them or be too difficult for them.
Other	Services directed at parents, such as parenting support, stabilizing services, guidance and meetings about parenting; children as victims of crime; other statements that did not fall under any of the other codes.
Risk	Situations when there is serious or acute imminent risk to the child; an acute emergency or crisis, violence, assault, serious physical abuse or sexual abuse and children need to be removed to be safe.

Chapter 3

I analyzed 67 responses to one interview question: 'Are there situations when it would not be appropriate to involve children in child protection-related processes?'. Twenty-eight study participants in Norway and 39 participants in California responded to this question. Table A.1 describes the codes that I used to write about non-involvement triggers in Chapter 3.

Chapter 4

I analyzed the responses of the 28 workers in Norway and 39 (out of a total of 40) workers in California who responded to the interview question: 'Can you tell me about a situation where the child's opinion mattered a lot to your decision?'. In my analysis of the participants' responses, I looked for thematic patterns related to the child's involvement in the case, the specific context of the case, and the way in which workers described the child and the child's parent(s) based on what I had learned from previous research (discussed in Chapter 2). I decided on six overarching themes that I coded as 'case context', 'child's age', 'child's communication of opinion', 'child's desperation

Table A.2: Code descriptions for Chapter 4

Code	Content
Case context	These are quotations that describe what kind of case it is, such as emotional, physical or sexual abuse; that the parents abuse alcohol and/or drugs; and that the situation the worker describes is a removal situation or a decision about parental visitations.
Child's age	This code encompasses statements related to the child's age, either mentioning the specific age or 'pre-teens', 'teens', or 'youth' when referring to adolescents.
Child's clear or credible communication	Statements that express that the child articulated clearly or credibly what had happened to them or expressed their opinion clearly, insistently, persistently and strongly; that the child's statement was credible, convincing, consistent, detailed, sensible or specific. This code includes statements about verbal communication (statements, dialogue, talking) and non-verbal communication (through actions such as running away from home).
Child's despair or fear	Statements that describe situations when the child felt distress or fear or was becoming desperate or depressed because of their home situation.
Evidence	This code encompasses statements that support what the child was saying or what the child wanted; this evidence could be physical evidence, such as bruises or scratches on a child's body, statements by other family members or professionals or experts who interacted with the child, or the worker's own observations of the child interacting with their parents in a meeting; it could consist of a history of interactions between the family and the child protection system. It includes statements of workers saying they did not have any other evidence than the child's statement.
Workers' perception of child or parent	This code included statements about the study participant perceiving the child as being honest, strong or mature on the one hand, or lying or manipulative on the other hand.

or fear', 'evidence' and 'worker's labelling of child and parent(s) or caregiver(s)'. Table A.2 shows the code descriptions for Chapter 4.

Chapters 5 and 6

I used the responses of 28 child protection workers in Norway and 40 workers in California for the analysis for Chapters 5 and 6. I analyzed the responses to two interview questions: 'At which stages in a case do you involve children?' and 'If your opinion about a case is different from the child's opinion, how do you proceed?'. (Depending on the worker's role, the first question was often followed up with how workers involved children in investigations, meetings, and so on.) Three of the

Table A.3: Code descriptions for Chapters 5 and 6

Code	Content
Child's age	This code includes statements about a child's age, including quotations such as "I've worked with youth now for several years" or "It depends on the child's age". It includes quotations saying that age is important to how a worker involves a child or highlights the difference in behaviour between younger and older children.
Facilitating participation	Quotations about how workers create or provide opportunities for children to develop their own opinion and/or express or voice their opinions and wishes.
Gathering information	Statements about how workers gather information from a child or evidence during an investigation.
Lying and manipulating children	Statements expressing that children "tell stories", lie or manipulate the parents and child protection agency to get away from their parents' supervision, or to satisfy their consumption desires or be able to engage in high-risk behaviours.
Providing information	These are quotations about providing information or explanations to children (about their right to a spokesperson, about the case process, and so on) and statements about workers explaining their opinions and decisions to children: why they think children need to be removed from home and placed into an out-of-home placement, should have a certain number or kind of visitation, need to go into substance use disorder treatment, and so on.

28 study participants in Norway were not asked the question about stages (N5, N22 and N27). One Norwegian participant was not asked the question about differences in opinion (N20). Two Californian participants out of 40 were not asked about stages (C17 and C23), and three were not asked about differences in opinion (C11, C29 and C37). Only one of the workers in the sample (N20) who was asked only one question (the one about stages) did not mention any specific involvement approach but did mention that she talked with children during an investigation almost from the beginning. Table A.3 shows the code descriptions for Chapters 5 and 6.

Limitations and strengths

In California, there were 10,485 public child protection workers in 2011. This includes full-time, part-time and temporary staff (California Social Work Education Center, 2011). The total number of employees working in the Norwegian child protection system amounted to 5,296 in 2017 (Statistics Norway, 2018). A total of 68 child protection workers were interviewed for this study. The data, which are derived from a self-selected group of workers in two municipalities in Norway and two counties in California, is clearly not representative of the general population of child protection caseworkers employed in public child protection agencies in Norway and California, let alone the US, where each state has its own regulations and practices (Berrick Duerr, 2011). Another limitation resulted from the skew of the Californian sample towards investigating workers in comparison with Norway, where, as I explained previously, workers' roles were more evenly divided between investigators and ongoing workers because recruitment in California occurred in emergency response units. This could have skewed the findings towards workers' conceptualizations of information gathering *from* children, rather than providing information *to* children (see Križ and Skivenes, 2011).

I have triangulated my findings with other relevant research in Norway, the US and other countries as discussed in Chapter 2. I also related my findings to the findings of other empirical studies on Norway and California at the end of each chapter and in the conclusion of the book.

One strength of the study is that we reached data saturation based on the number of interviews we conducted. The interviews yielded rich data that provided thick descriptions of concrete situations and cases related to children's participation that allowed me to detect clearly distinguishable themes. Another strength is that the study draws on a unique dataset about child protection workers in countries with different child protection systems and welfare systems. It is the only qualitative book-length study to date that compares child protection workers' experiences with children's participation in a protection-oriented child protection system (California) to those in a family service-oriented system (Norway).

APPENDIX 2

Discussion questions

Introduction

1. Why are the questions this study addresses important to the field of social work in general?
2. What were the motivations behind this study?
3. Can this research contribute to changing the class, racial/ethnic inequalities in the child protection system?
4. What do you see as the main differences between the child protection systems of Norway and the United States?
5. How would you describe the child protection system of your country when it comes to children's participation in child protection law, policy and practice?
6. How can the theories that underpin this study be useful to understanding children's participation in the organization you are working in?

Chapter 2

1. What do you learn about children's experiences with participation from this chapter?
2. What are the barriers to children's participation?
3. What are the practices that promote children's participation?
4. Have you experienced or seen these barriers and pathways to participation in your life or practice?
5. What has your organization done to deal with participation barriers?

Chapters 3 and 4

1. What are the factors that promote and hinder children's participation in child protection?
2. Have you experienced other participation and non-participation triggers in your practice?
3. How can social workers ensure their perceptions of children and young people are accurate?

Chapter 5

1. How did child protection caseworkers 'do participation' in Norway and the US?
2. How did case context, especially the particular stage of a case, matter to how child protection caseworkers did participation?
3. What do you think are other strategies to promote children's and young people's participation in the field of social work?

Chapter 6

1. How do you view younger and older children in terms of their capacities and skills to participate in decisions?
2. If you work with adolescents in your practice, what is the main takeaway from this chapter for you?
3. Have you ever taken the Implicit Association Test (IAT)? You can find more details at: www.youtube.com/watch?v=hr9xAcWv790. The actual test can be taken at https://implicit.harvard.edu/implicit/takeatest.html.

Chapter 7

1. Which findings do you find most useful for social work practice?
2. How could the study's findings be implemented in your practice?
3. How could you implement the idea of intersectionality in your practice?
4. If you replicated this study in your region or country, what do you think you would find?
5. Given the findings of this study, where would you take future research?
6. How do you think law, policy and practice in your country would need to change to allow for children's genuine participation?

Research methods

1. What is your (positive and negative) critique of the study design?
2. Which interview questions would you ask in a study on child protection caseworkers' experiences with children's participation?
3. How might the study samples have influenced the study findings? What if the study participants had all been ongoing caseworkers? What if they had been less experienced?

Notes

Chapter 1

1 All the names of the study participants in this book are pseudonyms to keep participants' identity anonymous.
2 The interviews for this study were conducted in California because the project's academic network helped facilitate access to study sites there.
3 These are workers with at least two years' experience and who directly interact with clients in their work.
4 Berrick Duerr's (2018) book on *Impossible Imperatives* in child protection highlights the tension between the paternalistic imperative of the child protection system and children's participation.
5 In the context of Finland, Pösö and Enroos (2017) have shown that children's views are only narrowly represented in court, and that the views of some children are not heard at all.
6 I am grateful to one of the anonymous reviewers of the book for pointing this out.
7 A study by Berrick Duerr and Skivenes (2012) about high-quality foster carers in Norway and the US suggests that the challenges faced by foster parents were similar in both countries.
8 The child population of 0 to 17-year-olds amounted to 1,111,776 children in Norway in 2016 (Statistics Norway, 2017b).
9 The total population of that age group (under 21 years old) in the US in 2016 was an estimated 86,638,615 individuals (calculations mine, based on the US Census, 2016).
10 Research comparing child protection workers' risk assessments has corroborated the existence of these different orientations by showing that public child protection workers differently assess risk and make decisions about out-of-home placements in Norway and the US (Križ and Skivenes, 2013; Skivenes and Stenberg, 2015). Scholars have noted that the US child protection system has moved in the direction of a family service orientation, for example through the introduction of differential (or alternative) response systems (Gilbert et al, 2011).

Chapter 2

1 The term 'contested practice' builds on the idea of 'essentially contested concepts' as developed by the Scottish philosopher Gallie (1956), who provided a radical critique of the idea of the objective nature of concepts (Schwartz, 1992). Gallie refers to concepts used by social scientists, such as art, democracy and social justice, as concepts whose definitions are a matter of dispute by those who use them because of the essential structure of the concepts themselves, which preclude a fixed definition and implementation (Schwartz, 1992). Social scientists inconsistently apply these kinds of concepts because of confusion or disputes about what they mean (Collier et al, 2006).
2 For a thorough review of the literature on barriers across western countries, see van Bijleveld et al (2014).
3 Most of the teens interviewed by Burford and Gallagher (2015) viewed their removals as traumatic.

4 However, Vis and Fossum (2015) noted that the difference might be explained by the different characteristics of the two groups of children – children living in residential care may be more vulnerable and have more serious mental health-related problems.

Chapter 4

1 The children whose cases the study participants discussed remained anonymous because none of the workers revealed their identity.

2 I analyzed whether workers talked about one gender more so than others but did not find this to be the case. A few workers mentioned children and youth whose parents were first generation immigrants and a few discussed young people's sexuality, but none of the workers mentioned the racial background of children and young people.

Chapter 5

1 None of the participants stated that they did not involve children. Out of the 28 Norwegian study participants, there were five (N9, N13, N18, N20 and N29) who did not discuss any specific approaches to participation in their responses but gave more general answers; for example, they simply stated that they listened to children (N29); that they "have contact with and speak with the child" (N9); that it depends on the case at which stage the worker involves the child (N13); that "occasionally we talk with the kids together with their parents" (N18); and that the worker talks with children almost from the beginning of an investigation (N20). All these participants except for N20 were asked both interview questions. N20 was not asked the question about differences in opinion; this participant may have provided a more specific response had she been asked the question about divergence of opinion with the child.

Chapter 6

1 I am thankful to an anonymous reviewer for pointing out the probable link between the character of the US child protection system and caseworkers' focus on figuring out whether a child is lying.

Chapter 7

1 Today's middle-class and wealthy children in the Global North often enjoy a sense of entitlement in interactions with professionals (Lareau, 2002; 2012) and empowerment as consumers (Schor, 2005).

2 Many of the children who encounter child protection agencies are from low-income families. Prior research has demonstrated a positive correlation between child maltreatment, family poverty and social inequality (see Cancian et al, 2010; Berger et al, 2013; Eckenrode et al, 2014).

References

Advokids (2018). Dependency court process. Retrieved from www.advokids.org/legal-tools/juvenile-court-process/.

Alderson, P. (2008). *Young children's rights: Exploring beliefs, principles and practice*. London: Jessica Kingsley Publishers.

Alfageme, E., Cantos, R. & Martinez, M. (2003). *De la participación al protagonismo infantil: Propuestas para la acción*. Madrid: Plataforma de Organizaciones de Infancia.

Arbeiter, E. & Toros, K. (2017). Participatory discourse: Engagement in the context of child protection assessment practices from the perspectives of child protection workers, parents and children. *Children and Youth Services Review*, 74, 17–27.

Archard, D. & Skivenes, M. (2009a). Balancing a child's best interests and a child's views. *International Journal of Children's Rights*, 17, 1–21.

Archard, D. & Skivenes, M. (2009b). Hearing the child. *Child and Family Social Work*, 14, 391–9.

Arnstein, S. (1969). A ladder of citizen participation. *Journal of the American Planning Association*, 35(4), 216–24.

Arts, W. & Gelissen, J. (2002). Three worlds of welfare capitalism or more? A state-of-the-art report. *European Journal of Social Policy*, 12(12), 137–58.

Bacon, K. & Frankel, S. (2014). Rethinking children's citizenship: Negotiating structure, shaping meanings. *International Journal of Children's Rights*, 22(1), 21–42.

Balsells, M. Á., Fuentes-Peláez, N. & Pastor, C. (2017). Listening to the voices of children in decision-making: A challenge for the child protection system in Spain. *Children and Youth Services Review*, 79, 418–25.

Barnes, E. W., Khoury, A. & Kelly, K. (2012). *Seen, heard, and engaged: Children in dependency court hearings*. Reno, NV: National Council of Juvenile and Family Court Judges.

Barnevernsproffene. (2011). *Det gode barnevernet: Stortingsmelding nr. 1 fra barn og unge i Norge*. Oslo: Forandringsfabrikken.

Barth, R. P., Lloyd, E. C., Christ, S., Chapman, M. & Dickinson, N. (2008). Child welfare worker characteristics and job satisfaction: A national study. *Social Work*, 53(3), 199–209.

Bårdsen, A. (2015). Children's rights in Norwegian courts. Seminar on Children's Rights, Kathmandu: 25 June.

Bell, M. (2002). Promoting children's rights through the use of relationship. *Child and Family Social Work*, 7(1), 1–11.

Berger, L. M., Font, S. A., Slack, K. S. & Waldfogel, J. (2013). Income and child maltreatment: Evidence from the Earned Income Tax Credit. Paper prepared for presentation at the 2013 Annual Meeting of the Association of Public Policy Analysis and Management, Washington, DC, 7–9 November.

Berrick Duerr, J. (2011). Trends and issues in the US child welfare system. In N. Gilbert, N. Parton & M. Skivenes, *Child protection systems: International trends and orientations* (pp 17–35). New York: Oxford University Press.

Berrick Duerr, J. (2018). *Impossible imperatives.* Berkeley, CA: University of California Press.

Berrick Duerr, J. & Skivenes, M. (2012). Dimensions of high quality foster care: Parenting plus. *Children and Youth Services Review, 34,* 1956–65.

Berrick Duerr, J., Dickens, J., Pösö, T. & Skivenes, M. (2015a). Children's involvement in care order decision-making: A cross-country analysis. *Child Abuse and Neglect, 49,* 128–41.

Berrick Duerr, J., Peckover, S., Pösö, T. & Skivenes, M. (2015b). The formalized framework for decision-making in child protection care orders: A cross-country analysis. *Journal of European Social Policy, 25*(4), 366–78.

Berrick Duerr, J., Dickens, J., Pösö, T. & Skivenes, M. (2017). Parents' involvement in care order decisions: A cross-country study of front-line practice. *Child and Family Social Work, 22,* 626–7.

Berrick Duerr, J., Dickens, J., Pösö, T. & Skivenes, M. (2018). International perspectives on child-responsive courts. *International Journal of Children's Rights, 26,* 251–77.

BLD. (2009). *Snakk med meg! En veileder om å snakke med barn i barneveret.* Oslo: Barne-og likestillingsdepartmentet.

Block, S., Oran, H., Oran, D., Baumrind, N. & Goodman, G. S. (2010). Abused and neglected children in court: Knowledge and attitudes. *Child Abuse and Neglect, 34*(9), 659–70.

Bourdieu, P. (1992). *The logic of practice.* Cambridge: Polity.

Brodkin, E. Z. (2012). Reflections on street-level bureaucracy: Past, present, and future. *Public Administration Review, 72*(6), 940–9.

Burford, G. & Gallagher, S. (2015). Teen experiences of exclusion, inclusion and participation in child protection and youth justice in Vermont. In T. Gal & B. F. Duramy, *International perspectives and empirical findings on child participation. From social exclusion to child-inclusive policies* (pp 227–55). London: Oxford University Press.

California Courts. (2019). California Rules of Courts. Retrieved from www.courts.ca.gov/rules.htm.

California Department of Social Services. (2010). *All county information notice no. I-24-10*, 26 March. Retrieved from www.cdss.ca.gov/lettersnotices/entres/getinfo/acin/2010/I-24_10.pdf.

California Department of Social Services. (2012). *Structured decision making*. Retrieved from www.childsworld.ca.gov/pg1332.htm.

California Social Work Education Center. (2011). *The 2011 California public child welfare workforce study: The population demographics and education levels*. Berkeley, CA: University of California, Berkeley.

California Social Work Education Center. (2012). *Statewide county public child welfare response to economic conditions*. Berkeley, CA: University of California, Berkeley. Retrieved from http://calswec-archive.berkeley.edu/sites/default/files/uploads/pdf/CalSWEC/CalSWEC/workforce_econ_conds.pdf.

Californian Department of Healthcare Services. (2017). *Frequently asked questions for child and family teams*. Retrieved from www.dhcs.ca.gov/formsandpubs/Documents/MHSUDS%20Information%20Notices/CFT_FAQs_ACL16-84_MHSUDIN16-049(3).pdf.

California Youth Connection. (2020). Legislative achievements. Retrieved from https://calyouthconn.org/leadership-in-action/legislative-achievements/.

Cancian, M., Shook Slack, K. & Young, Y. M. (2010). *The effect of family income on risk of child maltreatment*. Madison, WI: Institute for Research on Poverty.

Casey Family Programs (2019). Strategy brief: Healthy organizations. How was Safety Organized Practice implemented in San Diego County? Retrieved from www.casey.org/safety-organized-practice/.

Child Welfare Information Gateway. (2008). *An individualized, strengths-based approach in public child welfare driven systems of care*. Retrieved from www.childwelfare.gov/pubs/acloserlook/strengthsbased/strengthsbased1/.

Child Welfare Information Gateway. (2018). *State vs. county administration of child welfare services*. Retrieved from www.childwelfare.gov/pubs/factsheets/services/.

Collier, D., Hidalgo, F. D. & Maciuceanu, A. O. (2006). Essentially contested concepts: Debates and applications. *Journal of Political Ideologies, 11*(3), 211–46.

Collins, P. H. (1993). Toward a new vision: Race, class and gender as categories of analysis and connection. *Race, Sex and Class, 1*(1), 25–45.

Collins, R. & Makowsky, M. (2009). *The discovery of society*. Boston, MA: McGraw Hill.

Cossar, J., Brandon, M. & Jordan, P. (2014). "You've got to trust her and she's got to trust you": Children's views on participation in the child protection system. *Child and Family Social Work*, *21*(1), 103–12.

Crenshaw, K. (1989). Demarginalizing the intersectionality of race and sex: A Black feminist critique of antidiscrimination doctrine, feminist theory and antiracist politics. *University of Chicago Legal Forum*, *1*, 139–68.

D'Andrade, A., Austin, M. J. & Benton, A. (2008). Risk and safety assessment in child welfare: Instrument comparisons. *Journal of Evidence-Based Social Work*, *5*(1/2), 31–56.

Dahlø Husby, I. S., Slettebø, T. & Juul, R. (2018). Partnerships with children in child welfare: The importance of trust and pedagogical support. *Child and Family Social Work*, *23*, 443–50.

Doek, J. E. (2008). Foreword. In A. Invernizzi & J. Williams, *Children and Citizenship* (pp xii–xiv). London: Sage.

Dominelli, L. (2018). *Anti-racist social work*. London: Red Globe Press.

Douglas, M. (1966). *Purity and danger*. London: Routledge and Kegan Paul.

Eckenrode, J., Smith, E. G., McCarthy, M. E. & Dineen, M. (2014). Income inequality and child maltreatment in the United States. *Pediatrics*, *133*(3), 454–61.

Eidhammer, S. (2014). *Youth and participation in the child welfare service*. Masters thesis. Norway: NTNU.

Esping-Andersen, G. (1990). *The three worlds of welfare capitalism*. Cambridge: Polity Press.

Festinger, T. (1983). *No one ever asked us: A postscript to foster care*. New York: Columbia University Press.

Forandringsfabrikken (2018a). Presentation on *Forandringsfabrikken* at the Bergen Exchanges. University of Bergen, Centre for Law and Social Transformation: August.

Forandringsfabrikken (2018b) Presentation of The Change Factory by young pros. Porto, EUSARF: 4 October.

Fox, A. & Berrick Duerr, J. (2006). A response to No One Ever Asked Us: A review of children's experiences in out-of-home care. *Child and Adolescent Social Work Journal*, *24*(1), 23–51.

Fuentes-Peláez, N., Mateos, A., Balsells, M. A. & Rodrigo, M. J. (2018). The methodology of art-based research as a way to encourage child participation. Presentation at EUSARF conference, 3 October. Porto, Portugal.

Gallie, W. B. (1956). Essentially contested concepts. *Proceedings of the Aristotelian Society*, *56*, 167–98.

Gaytá, A. (1998). *Protagonismo infantil*. Retrieved from *La participación de niños y adolescentes en el contexto de la convención sobre los derechos del niño: Visiones y perspectivas*: www.unicef-irc.org/publications/pdf/bogota.pdf.

Gilbert, N., Parton, N. & Skivenes, M. (2011). Changing patterns of response and emerging orientations. In N. Gilbert, N. Parton & M. Skivenes, *Child protection systems: International trends and orientations* (pp 243–57). New York: Oxford University Press.

Glenn, E. N. (2010). Constructing citizenship: Exclusion, subordination and resistance. *American Sociological Review*, 76(1), 1–24.

Goffman, E. (1959). *The presentation of self in everyday life*. New York: Doubleday and Anchor.

Goldbeck, L., Laib-Koehnemund, A. & Fegert, J. (2007). Why social workers do not implement decisions to remove children at risk from home. A randomized controlled trial of consensus-based child abuse management. *Child Abuse and Neglect*, 31(9), 919–33.

Goldman, J. Salus, M. K., Wolcott, D. & Kennedy, K. Y. (2003). *A coordinated response to child abuse and neglect: The foundation for practice*. US Department of Health and Human Services. Administration for Children and Families Administration on Children, Youth and Families. Children's Bureau: Office on Child Abuse and Neglect.

Granosik, M., Gulczyńska, A., Kostrzyńska, M. & Littlechild, B. (2019). *Participatory social work: Research, practice, education*. New York: Columbia University Press.

Handley, D. & Doyle, C. (2008). Giving young children a voice in legal proceedings. *XVIIth ISPCAN International Congress*. Hong Kong: China SAR.

Haney, L. (1996). Homeboys, babies, men in suits: The state and the reproduction of male dominance. *American Sociological Review*, 61(5), 759–79.

Haney, L. (2002). *Inventing the needy: Gender and the politics of welfare in Hungary*. Berkeley, CA: University of California Press.

Hart, R. (1992). *Children's participation: From tokenism to citizenship*. UNICEF International Child Development Center. Retrieved from www.unicef-irc.org/publications/pdf/childrens_participation.pdf.

Healy, K. & Darlington, Y. (2009). Service user participation in diverse child protection contexts: Principles for practice. *Child and Family Social Work*, 14, 420–30.

Heggdalsvik, I. & Barmen Tysnes, I. (2018). Documentation of children's voice and participation in child welfare services: From idea to product. Presentation at EUSARF conference, 5 October. Porto, Portugal.

Hochman, G., Hochman, A. & Miller, J. (2004). *Foster care: Voices from the inside.* Retrieved from www.pewtrusts.org/en/research-andanalysis/reports/2004/02/18/voices-from-the-inside-foster-care.

Holland, S. & O'Neill, S. (2006). "We had to be there to make sure it is what we wanted": Enabling children's participation in family decision-making through the family group conference. *Childhood,* *13*(1), 91–111.

Honneth, A. (1996). *The struggle for recognition: The moral grammar of social conflicts.* Cambridge, MA: MIT Press.

Hunt, L. (2007). *Inventing human rights: A history.* New York: W. W. Norton.

Invernizzi, A. & Williams, J. (2008). Introduction. In A. Invernizzi & J. Williams, *Children and citizenship* (pp 1–7). London: Sage.

James, A. & Prout, A. (eds). (1997). *Constructing and reconstructing childhood: Contemporary issues in the sociological study of childhood.* London: Falmer Press.

James, A., Curtis, P. & Birch, J. (2008). Care and control in the construction of children's citizenship. In A. Invernizzi & J. Williams, *Children and Citizenship* (pp 85–96). London: Sage.

Jones, A. (2016, 28 January). After I lived in Norway, America felt backward. Here's why. A crash course in social democracy. *The Nation,* n.p. Retrieved from www.thenation.com/article/after-i-lived-in-norway-america-felt-backward-heres-why/.

Katz, I. (ed). (1997). *Approaches to empowerment and participation in child protection.* Chichester: John Wiley.

Knag Fylkesnes, M., Taylor, J. & Iversen, A. (2018). Precarious participation: Exploring ethnic minority youth's narratives about out-of-home placement in Norway. *Children and Youth Services Review,* *88*, 341–7.

Korteweg, A. C. (2006). The construction of gendered citizenship at the welfare office: An ethnographic comparison of welfare-to-work workshops in the United States and the Netherlands. *Social Politics,* *13*(3), 313–40.

Križ, K. & Roundtree-Swain, D. (2017). "We are merchandise on a conveyer belt": How young adults in the public child protection system perceive their participation in decisions about their care. *Children and Youth Services Review,* 32–40.

Križ, K. & Skivenes, M. (2013). Systemic differences in views on risk: A comparative case vignette study of risk assessment in England, Norway and the United States (California). *Children and Youth Services Review,* *35*, 1862–70.

Križ, K. & Skivenes, M. (2015). Child welfare workers' perceptions of children's participation: A comparative study of England, Norway and the USA. *Child and Family Social Work*, *11*(S2), 11–22.

Križ, K., Slayter, E., Iannicelli, A. & Lourie, J. (2012). Fear management. *Children and Youth Services Review*, *34*, 316–23.

Kvello, Ø. (2010). *Barn i risiko*. Oslo: Gyldendal.

Lamont, M. & Molnar, V. (2002). The study of boundaries in the social sciences. *Annual Review of Sociology*, *28*, 167–95.

Lamont, M., Pendergrass, S. & Pachucki, M. (2015). Symbolic boundaries. *International Encyclopedia of the Social and Behaviorial Sciences*, *23*, 850–5.

Lansdown, G. (2010). The realization of children's participation rights: Critical reflections. In B. Percy-Smith & N. Thomas, *A handbook of children and young people's participation: Perspectives from theory and practice* (pp 11–23). London: Routledge.

Lareau, A. (2002). Invisible inequality: Social class and childrearing in black families and white families. *American Sociological Review*, *67*(5), 747–76.

Lareau, A. (2012). *Unequal childhoods. Class, race, and family life*. Berkeley, CA: University of California Press.

Leeson, C. (2007). My life in care: Experiences of non-participation in decision-making processes. *Child and Family Social Work*, *12*, 268–77.

Lehmann, S., Havik, O. E., Havik, T. & Heiervang, E. R. (2013). Mental disorders in foster children: A study of prevalence, comorbidity and risk factors. *Child and Adolescent Psychiatry and Mental Health*, 7(39). Retrieved from https://capmh.biomedcentral.com/track/pdf/10.1186/1753-2000-7-39.

Lipsky, M. (1980). *Street-level bureaucracy: Dilemmas of the individual in public service*. New York: Russell Sage Foundation.

Lister, R. (2006). Children (but not women) first: New Labour, child welfare and gender. *Critical Social Policy*, *26*, 315–35.

Lister, R. (2008). Unpacking children's citizenship. In A. Invernizzi & J. Williams, *Children and citizenship* (pp 9–19). London: Sage.

Lofland, J., Snow, D., Anderson, L. & Lofland, L. (2006). *Analyzing social settings. A guide to qualitative observation and analysis*. Belmont, CA: Thomson Wadsworth.

Magnussen, A.-M. & Skivenes, M. (2015). The child's opinion and position in care order proceedings: An analysis of judiciary discretion in the county boards' decision-making. *International Journal of Children's Rights*, 705–23.

Mateos, A., Vaquero, E., Balsells, M. A. & Pomce, C. (2017). "They didn't tell me anything: they just sent me home": Children's participation in the return home. *Child and Family Social Work, 22,* 871–80.

Maxwell, J. (2005). *Qualitative research design: An interactive approach.* Thousand Oaks, CA: Sage.

Ministry of Children and Equality. (2016). *The Rights of the Child in Norway. Norway's fifth and sixth periodic reports to the UN Committee on the Rights of the Child – 2016.* Retrieved from www.regjeringen. no/globalassets/departementene/bld/rapport-fns-barnekonvensjon-2016.pdf.

Ministry of Children, Equality and Social Inclusion. (2017). *Act of 17 July 1992 No. 100 relating to Child Welfare Services (the Child Welfare Act).* Retrieved from www.regjeringen.no/contentassets/049114cce 0254e56b7017637e04ddf88/the-norwegian-child-welfare-act.pdf.

Moldestad, B., Havik, T. & Backe-Hansen, E. B. (1998). *Barnets talsperson: En evaluering av ordningen med barnets talsperson (An evaluation of the child advocacy programme).* Bergen: BVU-Vestlandet.

Naddeo, L. & Vidiz, M. (2018). Making My History project – A tool for children's and young people's participation in child welfare decisions. Presentation at EUSARF conference, 5 October. Porto, Portugal: October.

Nord Sæbjørnsen, S. E. & Willumsen, E. (2017). Service user participation in interprofessional teams in child welfare in Norway: Vulnerable adolescents' perceptions. *Child and Family Social Work, 22*(S2), 43–53.

Norwegian Directorate for Children, Youth and Family Affairs (*Barne, Ungdoms og Familiedirektoratet*). (2010). *Brukerundersøkelse blandt barn i statlige og private barneverntiltak.* Oslo: Rambøll.

Norwegian Directorate for Children, Youth and Family Affairs. (2017). *The Norwegian child welfare services.* Retrieved from www.bufdir.no/ en/English_start_page/The_Norwegian_Child_Welfare_Services/.

OECD. (2017). *Alcohol consumption (indicator).* Retrieved from https:// data.oecd.org/healthrisk/alcohol-consumption.htm#indicator-chart.

Oppedal, M. (1999). *Rettsikerhet ved akutte vedtak etter barnevernloven (The rule of law in acute decisions uinder the Child Welfare Act).* Oslo: Universitetsforlaget.

Paulsen, V. (2015). *Children and youths' participation in the child welfare service. Presentation. NTNU Trondheim, Norway.* Retrieved from http://isci2015.org/docs/pdfs/4d/2%20Paulsen_Childrens%20 participation%20in%20the%20child%20welfare%20services%20 in%20Norway.pdf.

Paulsen, V. (2016). Ungdommers erfaringer med medvirkning i barneveret. *Fontene Forskning, 1*, 4–15.

Petersen, M. (2018). Children's participation in social work research and development: Openings, opportunities, obligations and considerations. Presentation at EUSARF conference, 5 October. Porto, Portugal: October.

Pinkney, S. (2011). Participation and emotions: Troubling encounters between children and social welfare professionals. *Children and Society, 25*, 37–46.

Piper, C. (2008). Will law think about children? Reflections on Youth Matters. In A. Invernizzi & J. Williams, *Children and Citizenship* (pp 147–57). London: Sage.

Pölkki, P., Vornanen, R., Pursiainen, M. & Riikonen, M. (2012). Children's participation in child-protection processes as experienced by foster children and social workers. *Child Care in Practice, 18*(2), 107–25.

Pösö, T. & Enroos, R. (2017). The representation of children's views in Finnish court decisions regarding care order. *International Journal of Children's Rights, 25*(3–4), 736–53.

Qvortrup, J. (1990). *Childhood as a social phenomenon: An introduction to a series of national reports. Eurosocial Report nr. 36.* Vienna: European Centre.

Qvortrup, J. (2009). Are children human beings or human becomings? A critical assessment of outcome thinking. *Rivista Internazionale di Scienze Sociali, 117*(3/4), 631–53.

Reed, D. & Karpilow, K. (2002). *Understanding the child welfare system in California: A primer for service providers and policy makers.* Berkeley, CA: California Center for Research on Women and Families. Retrieved from www.fiscalexperts.com/pdf_files/CWS_Primer.pdf.

Roberts, D. (2002). *Shattered bonds: The color of child welfare.* New York: Basics Civitas Books.

Roberts, D. (2008). The racial geography of child welfare: Toward a new research paradigm. *Child Welfare, 87*(2), 125–50.

Roberts, D. & Sangoi, L. K. (2018). *Black families matter: How the child welfare system punishes poor families of color.* Retrieved from *In Justice Today*: https://medium.com/in-justice-today/black-families-matter-how-the-child-welfare-system-punishes-poor-families-of-color-33ad20e2882e.

Ryan, S. Wiles, D. Cash, S. & Siebert, C. (2005). Risk assessments: Empirically supported or values driven? *Children and Youth Services Review, 27*(2), 213–25.

Sanders, R. & Mace, S. (2006). Agency policy and the participation of children and young people in the child protection process. *Child Abuse Review*, *15*, 89–109.

Schofield, G. & Thoburn, J. (1996). *Child protection: The voice of the child in decision-making*. London: Institute for Public Policy Research.

Schor, J. (2005). *Born to buy: The commercialized child and the new consumer culture*. New York: Scribner.

Schwartz, A. (1992). *Contested concepts in cognitive social science*. Retrieved from https://ulan.mede.uic.edu/~alansz/contested-concepts.pdf.

Shemmings, D. (2000). Professionals' attitudes to children's participation in decision-making: Dichotomous accounts and doctrinal contests. *Child and Family Social Work*, *3*, 235–43.

Shier, H. (2001). Pathways to participation: Openings, opportunities and obligations. *Children and Society*, *15*(2), 107–17.

Skivenes, M. (2011). Norway: Toward a child-centric perspective. In N. Gilbert, N. Parton & M. Skivenes, *Child protection systems: International trends and orientations* (pp 154–79). New York: Oxford University Press.

Skivenes, M. (2015). The space for children's participation (in Norwegian). *Tidsskrift for Velferdsforskning*, *1*, 48–60.

Skivenes, M. & Søvig, H. (2017). Child welfare decision-making in cases of removals of children. In K. Burns, T. Pösö & M. Skivenes, *Child welfare removals by the state* (pp 40–64). New York: Oxford University Press.

Skivenes, M. & Stenberg, H. (2015). Risk assessment and domestic violence – how do child welfare workers in three countries assess and substantiate the risk level of a 5-year-old girl? *Child and Family Social Work*, *20*, 424–36.

Skivenes, M. & Strandbu, A. (2006). A child perspective and children's participation. *Children, Youth and Environments*, *16*(2), 10–27.

Slayter, E. (2016). Youth with disabilities in the United States child welfare system. *Children and Youth Services Review*, *64*, 155–65.

Smith, A. B., Taylor, N. J. & Tapp, P. (2003). Rethinking children's involvement in decision-making after parental separation. *Childhood*, *10*, 201–16.

Smith, B. D. & Donovan, S. E. (2003). Child welfare practice in organizational and institutional context. *Social Service Review*, 541–63.

Social Security Act. (2006). Amended title IV-B reauthorizing the promoting safe and stable families program. Sec. 475 [42 U.S.C. 675].

Soerlie, H. (2018, 4 October). How can the child welfare services improve the child's participation in the assessment? Presentation at EUSARF conference, October. Porto, Portugal.

State of California Health and Human Services Agency. (2010). Team Decisionmaking Meetings (TDM) desk guide. Retrieved from www. cdss.ca.gov/lettersnotices/entres/getinfo/acin/2010/I-24_10.pdf.

Statistics Norway. (2015). *Children and adolescents with immigrant background in child welfare services 2012.* Retrieved from www.ssb. no/en/sosiale-forhold-og-kriminalitet/artikler-og-publikasjoner/ barn-og-unge-med-innvandrerbakgrunn-i-barnevernet-2012.

Statistics Norway. (2017a). *Child welfare 2015.* Retrieved from www. ssb.no/en/sosiale-forhold-og-kriminalitet/statistikker/barneverng/ aar/2016-07-01.

Statistics Norway. (2017b). *Families and households. Table 2. Children 0–17 years.* Retrieved from www.ssb.no/en/befolkning/statistikker/ familie.

Statistics Norway. (2018). *Child welfare.* Retrieved from www.ssb.no/ en/barneverng/.

Ten Brummelaar, M. D., Knorth, E. J., Post, W. J., Harder, A. T. & Kalverboer, M. E. (2016). Space between the borders? Perceptions of professionals on the participation in decision-making of young people in coercive care. *Qualitative Social Work, 17*(5), 692–711.

Ten Brummelaar, M. D., Harder, A. T., Kalverboer, M. E., Post, W. J. & Knorth, E. J., (2017). Participation of youth in decision-making procedures during residential care: A narrative review. *Child and Family Social Work, 23*(1), 33–44.

Thomas, N. (2002). *Children, family and the state: Decision-making and child participation.* Bristol: Policy Press.

Thomas, N. (2007). Towards a theory of children's participation. *International Journal of Children's Rights, 15*, 199–218.

Thomas, N. & O'Kane, C. (1999a). Children's participation in review and planning meetings when they are 'looked after' in middle childhood. *Child and Family Social Work, 4*, 221–30.

Thomas, N. & O'Kane, C. (1999b). Experiences of decision-making in middle childhood: The example of children 'looked after' by local authorities. *Childhood, 6*(3), 369–87.

Thomas, N. & Percy-Smith, B. (2012). "It's about changing services and building relationships": Evaluating the development of children in care councils. *Child and Family Social Work, 17*, 487–96.

Tregeagle, S. & Mason, J. (2008). Service user experience of participation in child welfare case management. *Child and Family Social Work, 13*, 391–401.

Turney, K. & Wildeman, C. (2016). Mental and physical health of children in foster care. *Pediatrics*, *138*(5). Retrieved from https://pediatrics.aappublications.org/content/pediatrics/138/5/e20161118.full.pdf.

UK Department for Education and Skills (2005). Youth matters: Next steps. Retrieved from https://dera.ioe.ac.uk/7254/17/ACFA64E_Redacted.pdf.

Ulvik, O. S. (2015). Talking with children: Professional conversations in a participation perspective. *Qualitative Social Work*, *14*(2), 193–208.

UNICEF (2013). *Innocenti report card 11*. Retrieved from *Child well-being in rich countries: A comparative review* at www.unicef.org.uk/Images/Campaigns/FINAL_RC11-ENGLORES-fnl2.pdf.

United Nations. (2020). Convention on the Rights of the Child. Retrieved from www.ohchr.org/en/professionalinterest/pages/crc.aspx.

United Nations Office on Drugs and Crime. (2011). *World drug report 2011*. Retrieved from www.unodc.org/documents/data-and-analysis/WDR2011/World_Drug_Report_2011_ebook.pdf.

United States Census. (2016). *Annual Estimates of the Resident Population by Single Year of Age and Sex for the United States: April 1, 2010 to July 1, 2016, 2016 Population Estimates*. Retrieved from https://factfinder.census.gov/faces/tableservices/jsf/pages/productvi.

US Department of Health and Human Services, Administration for Children and Families, Administration on Children, Youth and Families. (2017). *The AFCARS report*. Retrieved from www.acf.hhs.gov/sites/default/files/cb/afcarsreport24.pdf.

US Department of Health and Human Services, Administration for Children and Families, Administration on Children, Youth and Families, Children's Bureau. (2018a). *Child maltreatment 2016*. Retrieved from www.acf.hhs.gov/cb/research-data-technology/st.

US Department of Health and Human Services, Administration for Children and Families, Administration on Children, Youth and Families. (2018b). The risk and prevention of maltreatment of children with disabilities. A bulletin for professionals.

US Department of Health and Human Services. Children's Bureau. (2018). *The AFCARS report*. Retrieved from www.acf.hhs.gov/sites/default/files/cb/afcarsreport24.pdf

Van Bijleveld, G. G., Dedding, C. W. & Bunders-Aelen, J. F. (2014). Children's and young people's participation within child welfare and child protection services: A state-of-the-art review. *Child and Family Social Work*, *20*, 129–38.

Vis, S. A. (2004). *Samtaler med barn i barnevernet (Conversations with children in child welfare).* Skriftserie Barnevernets Utviklingssenter i Nord-Norge.

Vis, S. A. & Fossum, S. (2013). Representation of children's views in court hearings about custody and parental visitations: A comparison between what children wanted and the courts ruled. *Children and Youth Services Review, 35,* 2101–9.

Vis, S. A. & Fossum, S. (2015). Organizational factors and child participation in decision-making: Differences between two child welfare organizations. *Child and Family Social Work, 20,* 277–87.

Vis, S. A. & Thomas, N. (2009). Beyond talking: Children's participation in Norwegian care and protection cases. *European Journal of Social Work, 12*(2), 155–69.

Vis, S. A., Holtan, A. & Thomas, N. (2012). Obstacles for child participation in care and protection cases: Why Norwegian workers find it difficult. *Child Abuse Review, 21,* 7–23.

Vis, S. A., Strandbu, A., Holtan, A. & Thomas, N. (2011). Participation and health: A research review of child participation in planning and decision-making. *Child and Family Social Work, 16,* 325–35.

Wallace-Henry, C. (2015). Unveiling child sexual abuse through participatory action research. *Social and Economic Studies, 64*(1), 13–36.

Weber, M. (1946). Bureaucracy. In H. H. Gerth & C. W. Mills, *From Max Weber: Essays in sociology* (pp 196–244). New York: Oxford University Press.

Weiss, R. S. (1994). *Learning from strangers: The art and method of qualitative interview studies.* New York: Free Press.

Weisz, V., Wingrove, T., Beal, S. & Faith-Slaker, A. (2011). Children's participation in foster care hearings. *Child Abuse and Neglect, 35*(4), 267–72.

West, C. & Zimmerman, D. H. (1987). Doing gender. *Gender and Society, 1*(2), 125–51.

Willumsen, E. & Skivenes, M. (2005). Collaboration between service users and professionals: Legitimate decisions in child protection – a Norwegian model. *Child and Family Social Work, 10,* 197–206.

Woodhouse, B. B. (1992). "Who owns the child?": Meyer and Pierce and the child as property. *William and Mary Law Review,* 995–1122.

Zelizer, V. (1994). *Pricing the priceless child: The changing social value of children.* Princeton, NJ: Princeton University Press.

Index

Note: Page numbers in *italics* indicate figures and tables. Page numbers followed by 'n' refer to notes.

9781447355892